I0186927

Conservative Jewry in the United States:

A Sociodemographic Profile

Sidney Goldstein and Alice Goldstein

Produced under a grant from The Pew Charitable Trusts

This publication has been made possible through a grant from the
Mandell L. Berman and Madeleine H. Berman Foundation

A Project of The Ratner Center for the Study of Conservative Judaism
The Jewish Theological Seminary of America

Copyright © 1998, The Jewish Theological Seminary of America

Contents

List of Figures

Foreword

Conservative Jewry in the United States: A Sociodemographic Profile is the third in a series of publications emanating from the North American Study of Conservative Synagogues and Their Members. The larger study included three freshly commissioned surveys of congregational practices and programs, the behavior and beliefs of members, and the attitudes and practices of recent bar and bat mitzvah celebrants. All three of these surveys were conducted in 1995-96. In addition, two ethnographers each studied a pair of Conservative synagogues to learn more about the cultures of congregations. And a sociologist of American Protestant denominations situated the Conservative movement within the larger landscape of American religion.

In order to place these connected research projects into a broader framework, Sidney and Alice Goldstein undertook a detailed analysis of national and local survey data for the purpose of comparing self-identified Conservative Jews who are currently members of a synagogue with those who are currently not affiliated. They have also incorporated a fascinating comparison of Conservative Jews with American Jews who identify with other Jewish denominations or none at all. In the finest tradition of engaged scholarship, the Goldsteins herein present an honest and somewhat disturbing portrait of a religious movement in flux, which is accompanied by provocative suggestions for future policy planning within the Conservative movement.

The initial research for this project was undertaken under a grant from The Pew Charitable Trusts to the Ratner Center for the Study of Conservative Judaism at the Jewish Theological Seminary of America. All of us who have worked on this project are indebted to the Trusts' President, Rebecca Rimel, and her staff in the Religion Division for their support, as we are to the Seminary's Chancellor, Professor Ismar Schorsch, for his unflagging encouragement.

The Goldsteins' finding were initially reported in two earlier publications--**Conservative Synagogues and Their Members: Highlights of the North American Survey of 1995-96** and **Jewish Identity and Religious Commitment: The North American Study of Conservative Synagogues and Their Members, 1995-96**. This volume presents their complete report. Its publication has been made possible through the generosity of the Mandell L. and Madeleine H. Berman Foundation. The Bermans have a long history of sponsoring research on the current condition of the American Jewish community. We are grateful for their support of our work.

It is my pleasure to acknowledge the professionalism of Ben Davis who copy-edited the manuscript and Glenn L. Abel, the designer of this publication.

Jack Wertheimer, Project Director
The Ratner Center for the Study of Conservative Judaism
The Jewish Theological Seminary of America

Preface

As scholars who have been extensively involved in research on the American Jewish community and as Conservative Jews, we welcomed the invitation extended us by Professor Jack Wertheimer to participate in the North American Study of Conservative Synagogues and Their Members, undertaken by the Jewish Theological Seminary's Ratner Center for the Study of Conservative Judaism, with support from The Pew Charitable Trusts.

On a personal level, being Conservative Jews has been rewarding for us because of the movement's ideological commitment to maintaining Jewish tradition while confronting the challenges of modernization and rapid social change. At the same time, the wide discrepancies observed between the ideology of the movement and the religious practices of so many of its adherents have raised strong doubts about the denomination's long-term viability. We strongly believe it is urgent to understand these discrepancies better and to develop strategies for coping with them. Assessing the sociodemographic status of the Conservative population of the United States represented an important step toward this end, and we have been happy to contribute to such an endeavor. Our interest in doing so was reinforced by three other considerations.

1. The opportunity to base this report on data from the 1990 National Jewish Population Study (NJPS-90), sponsored by the Council of Jewish Federations, provided a strong confirmation of the value of NJPS-1990 for understanding the structure and dynamics of American Jewry. As scholars who had been intimately involved in the design, execution, and analysis of the NJPS-1990 data, we were aware of the richness of the data set and were delighted to see their use extended to this evaluation of the Conservative population.

2. Recognizing that most of the components of the JTS study were focusing on Conservative synagogues and their members, we believed strongly that the overall study must also take account of the large numbers of American Jews who consider themselves Conservative but who do not belong to a synagogue, since they constitute a majority of all those who identify as Conservative Jews. Without attention to this group and a fuller understanding of how they differ from the members in their socioeconomic characteristics, extent of Jewish practices, and involvement in the Jewish community, any study of Conservative Jewry would be incomplete and possibly even misleading. Moreover, fuller assessment of the nonaffiliated is a prerequisite for any efforts to attract them into fuller participation in synagogue life.

3. A study restricted to current Conservative Jews, whether synagogue members or not, does not allow full assessment of the dynamics of change within the Conservative population, since it does not include all those who dropped their Conservative identity in favor of other denominations, Christianity, or secularism. The data from NJPS-1990 permit such an evaluation of switching, not only into the movement but also out of it. In doing so, insights can be gained into what factors may be attracting or disaffecting individuals.

Motivated by all these concerns and taking advantage of the richness of NJPS-1990, this volume profiles Conservative Jewry in the United States in 1990 in comparison to those American Jews who identified with the Orthodox, Reform, or Reconstructionist denominations or who regarded themselves as secular. It devotes more in-depth attention to the Conservative population itself, with special focus on the differences in socioeconomic status and religious behavior associated with age and synagogue membership. Finally, it evaluates the extent and character of switching into and out of Conservative Jewry and the implications of past trends for the future vitality of the movement.

In undertaking this research, we have been greatly helped by a large number of colleagues and staff.

We are especially grateful to Dr. Jack Wertheimer, director of the study, for giving us the opportunity to participate in the project and for his encouragement and interest. His careful attention to earlier drafts of this report is greatly appreciated. The members of the project research team provided constructive suggestions for the design and analysis, as well as revisions, of the report; their insights have enriched our analysis.

Many individuals have contributed their expertise in providing the data on which our analyses are based. Jeff Scheckner, of the North American Jewish Data Bank, supplied the data sets used for analysis of individual communities; their statistical analysis was assisted by John Iceland and Sun Rongjun, graduate students in the Department of Sociology, Brown University. Irene Gravel was responsible for creating the computer files from NJPS-1990, which forms the basis of our report. Typing of statistical tables and creation of graphics were undertaken by Carol Walker and Thomas Alarie, both of whom are on the staff of the Population Studies and Training Center, Brown University. The work of these several individuals greatly facilitated our research, and we thank them for their important contributions.

Special recognition is due Mandell L. Berman for his continuing strong interest in and support of research on American Jewry. The subsidy he provided for publication of this report is gratefully acknowledged.

The interpretation of the data in our report is our own; it does not necessarily reflect the views of either other members of the Pew research team of the North American Study of Conservative Synagogues and Their Members or others associated with the Jewish Theological Seminary.

As committed Conservative Jews, we welcome the opportunity to provide this demographic profile of Conservative Jewry in the United States and hope that our analysis proves useful in efforts to enhance the vitality of the movement.

We dedicate this volume to the blessed memory of our parents, Bella and Max Goldstein and Greta and Fred Dreifuss, all of them immigrants from Europe. Bella and Max arrived among the large waves of immigrants who came from Eastern Europe in the early 1900s; Greta and Fred were among the refugees from Germany in the late 1930s, thus fortunately escaping the gas chambers. Their dedication to Jewish tradition and to the vitality of Judaism in America has been a continuous inspiration for us. It seems most appropriate that this volume, which focuses on some of the results of the transitions in American Judaism during the twentieth century and on the challenges of the twenty-first, be dedicated to their memory.

I. Introduction

Conservative Judaism evolved in response to the need to integrate the waves of East European immigrants into American life while enabling them to maintain their sense of ethnic and religious identity (Sklare, 1972). The new movement was particularly important as the immigrants moved out of their initial areas of settlement into other urban and then suburban localities. Conservative Judaism appealed to them not only because of their increasing Americanization, but also because of their changing class status from working-class origins to middle-class status as owners/managers of businesses and professionals.

The movement drew heavily from formerly Orthodox families, providing these new adherents to Conservative Judaism a familiar context combined with less stringent observances. In fact, one of the major contradictions Sklare identified in the Conservative movement was the chasm between the traditional stance of the rabbis, especially those at the Jewish Theological Seminary, on observance of Jewish law, especially kashrut and Shabbat observance, and the laxity of the Conservative lay members. Sklare also identified the autonomy of the individual congregations as exacerbating the lack of a centralized, coherent ideological position in Conservative Judaism that could apply broadly to both the clergy and the membership.

On a more positive note, by midcentury, Conservative congregations had developed religious schools to socialize and educate youth and to provide a cadre of future adherents. Congregations had also expanded their activities to encompass not only worship and education but also social programs that provided opportunities for association and voluntarism similar to that of nonsectarian organizations.

Sklare concluded that by 1950, "it does seem true that if Conservatism has had a 'historic mission' in terms of preventing the complete alienation and religious disorganization of the East European-derived Jew, that task has been completed" (Sklare, 1972:252). Unforeseen in the first edition of his study, but described in a 1972 edition, the 1950s and 1960s saw an unprecedented growth in the Conservative movement, which led to its primacy among the three major denominations. A major factor in the change was the dramatic movement of the population — Jewish and general — from cities to suburbs.

Suburbanization for Jews was accompanied by a massive spurt in the building of Conservative synagogues. While Orthodox synagogues largely remained in older areas of settlement, where Jewish population density allowed adherents to walk to services, and Reform congregations remained dependent on the temples they had built on city peripheries some decades earlier, the Conservative synagogue gained visual and numerical prominence in the rapidly growing suburbs. At the same time, the movement developed a series of auxiliary institutions, including the Ramah camps and some day schools, that strengthened the identification of lay people with the Conservative movement.

Nonetheless, the contradictions between official ideology and individual observance that Sklare had identified as characterizing the movement in the 1940s continued. Assimilation posed an increasing threat to continuity, and leaders of the movement questioned the appeal of Conservative Judaism to younger Jews. In the large metropolitan centers a significant number of Jews identified themselves as Conservative but remained unaffiliated. All that seemed necessary to further augment the primacy of Conservative Judaism, Sklare (1972:260-61) suggested, was that such individuals be induced to activate a commitment they already held. As our study shows, the problem remains two decades later. Whether the Conservative movement can, in fact, draw these individuals into active participation remains a key question.

Assuring the continuity and growth of Conservative Judaism requires a broad understanding of its constituents. As Sklare emphasized at the very outset of his study, "Changes in Judaism have their origin in changes in the lives of Jews" (Sklare, 1972:15). Knowing who identifies as Conservative and how closely their religious practices follow Conservative ideology is, therefore, a key to planning for the future. The movement recognized the importance of this strategy and undertook a self-study in 1979 (Shapiro, 1980). That study largely confirmed the findings of the 1970 National Jewish Population Survey (Massarick and Chenkin, 1973) and the 1975 Boston survey (Fowler, 1977): Conservative Jews held high educational and occupational status but were a relatively aging population. Although the movement had gained strongly from the Orthodox in the past, it was no longer doing so; in fact, it seemed to be losing the allegiance of members' children. Particular concerns were raised by the 1979 survey about the weakening commitment of second- and third-generation Conservative Jews. More positively, a strong correlation existed among affiliation, intensity of formal Jewish education, and extent of informal educational activities as exemplified by camping and youth groups.

Responses to the Shapiro survey findings were varied. They included an awareness of the need to strengthen Jewish education (especially the Schechter Day School movement), the compilation of a new prayer book *(Sim Shalom)*, and an in-depth examination of Conservative beliefs that were put forth in *Emet v'Emunah*. No systematic evaluation of the effects of these efforts was undertaken, however; and a sense of unease seems to have persisted even as the Jewish Theological Seminary celebrated its 100th anniversary in 1987 (Klagsbrun, 1987). Nor were systematic attempts made to discern if the trends identified in the 1979 survey were continuing through the 1980s. The sweeping and disruptive changes that occurred during the 1980s in American religious life in general — and which included American Jewry (Wertheimer, 1993) — made any predictions about the strength of a particular denomination particularly problematic.

Cognizant of the need for a thorough reassessment of Conservative Judaism at the end of the twentieth century, the Jewish Theological Seminary, with funding from The Pew Charitable Trust, has undertaken a broad, multifaceted study of the movement. Its emphasis is on understanding what helps foster a strong commitment to Conservative Judaism. This report is part of that larger study.

Using data from the 1990 National Jewish Population Survey (NJPS-1990), augmented by local community surveys undertaken in the 1980s, we provide a profile of persons in the United States who identify themselves as Conservative Jews. We delineate the sociodemographic profile of Conservative Jews, examine some of their religious/ritual behavior and beliefs, and assess the trends in movement into and out of Conservative Judaism. The data will, thereby, provide the basis for evaluating changes during the closing decades of the twentieth century and for planning and programming in the future.

The NJPS-1990 data have the great advantage of covering self-identified Conservative Jews who are both affiliated and unaffiliated with synagogues/temples. Most studies of a particular denomination, including earlier studies of Conservative Judaism, have relied almost exclusively on information provided by synagogues or on respondents drawn from synagogue membership lists. With affiliation rates at a low 41 percent nationally (Kosmin et al, 1991), a large segment of the population who identify themselves as adherents of a denomination are overlooked.

Our study makes full use of the NJPS-1990 data to examine the characteristics and behavior of Conservative Jews in the aggregate and to draw distinctions between the affiliated and the unaffiliated. An analysis of differences and similarities between these groups can be especially helpful in assessing the strength of the movement currently in terms of both the sociodemographic characteristics of its members and their commitment to Conservative ideology. It can also play a key role in planning future recruitment efforts or outreach programs.

The representativeness of the NJPS-1990 data also allows comparisons of the Conservative population with those identifying with other denominations or with no denomination. In this way, we will be able to determine the degree to which Conservative Jews are centrist or exceptional in the spectrum of American Jews in general. While most of our focus for this aspect of the analysis will be in comparison with Orthodox and Reform Jews, where possible we will also pay attention to Reconstructionist Jews and to those who identify as Just Jews or Other.

Despite the strengths of NJPS-1990, a full assessment of the sociodemographic and economic characteristics of Conservative Jewry in the United States and the impact these background characteristics have on Jewish identity and behavior requires far more information than is available from omnibus studies, either national or local. The wide range of topics encompassed by such surveys precludes any in-depth attention to particular topics, including that of denominational identity. NJPS-1990, however, and, in varying degrees, the local surveys we use include an important core set of questions on current and earlier denominational identity together with a wide array of information on other demographic, economic, and social variables, as well as on behavioral and attitudinal indicators of Jewish identity. NJPS-1990 thus offers the best opportunity yet available to assess Conservative Jewry and other denominations nationally, to gain insights into the extent of variability from community to community or regionally, and to evaluate changes in denominational identity.

Our discussion begins with a description of the basic characteristics of the denominations, focusing on differentials in membership, age, and regional distribution. We turn next to a more detailed examination of the sociodemographic profile of Conservative Jews in comparison to those of the Orthodox and Reform movements and other groups. Within the Conservative group we compare members and nonmembers. Subsequent sections examine the factors that enhance the likelihood of synagogue membership, synagogue attendance, and informal networks among Jews. In light of the major redistribution of Jews across the United States over the past four decades, we also analyze the migration experience of Conservative Jews and how that has changed their geographic configuration. This leads to a discussion of regional differences in characteristics and behavior. Finally, we discuss the direction of shifts in denominational identification and how these have affected the sociodemographic and religious composition of Conservative Jewry. A concluding section identifies the major themes that have emerged from our analysis and suggests some of their implications for the future of Conservative Jewry in the United States.

II. Some Basic Features

The overwhelming majority of adult Jews in the United States identify with one of the four major religious denominations of American Judaism — Orthodox, Conservative, Reform, and Reconstructionist. According to NJPS-1990, 80 percent of adult Jews[1] did so, somewhat lower than the 86 percent reported by the 1970/71 National Jewish Population Study. In 1990, 10 percent of adult Jewish Americans considered themselves as Just Jewish, and almost as many specified no denominational identity.

The high proportion who report a denominational affiliation surely points to the importance of denominational identity as a force in American Jewish life. It suggests that religious denomination constitutes a major dimension along which the American Jewish community subdivides itself. To the extent that denominational affiliation correlates with a given set of attitudes and practices, it has great relevance for the character of American Judaism. Whether, in fact, such correlations are strong or weak will be examined as part of the larger analysis undertaken here in order to assess whether denominational boundaries are clear-cut or diffused and to what extent they point to sharp or weak divisions within the larger community.

To determine the denominational distribution of the American Jewish population, NJPS-1990 asked all respondents: "Referring to Jewish religious denominations do you consider yourself to be Conservative, Orthodox, Reform, Reconstructionist, or something else?" The wide range of responses in addition to the four specified denominations reflects the religious heterogeneity of the American Jewish community in the 1990s. An estimated 1,588,000 Jewish adults identified as Conservative (Table A), constituting 35 percent of the total adult Jewish population (Figure 1). They were slightly surpassed by adults who indicated they were Reform, 38 percent of the total. The Orthodox constituted only 6 percent of Jewish adults, and those who identified as Reconstructionist were just over 1 percent.

The denominational profile of the Jewish population varies considerably, however, from community to community, with Conservative and Reform alternating between being the largest and second largest denomination. Among the communities we have included for analysis, for example, Conservative Jews are predominant

---

1. When discussing the findings of NJPS-1990, we refer to the "core" Jewish population, defined as Jews by religion, Jews by choice, or secular Jews (Kosmin et al, 1991); here we refer to this population as Jews. Excluded from most of the analyses are those persons encompassed in NJPS-1990 who were of Jewish descent, but not Jewish at the time of the survey; they are included when we discuss denominational switching.

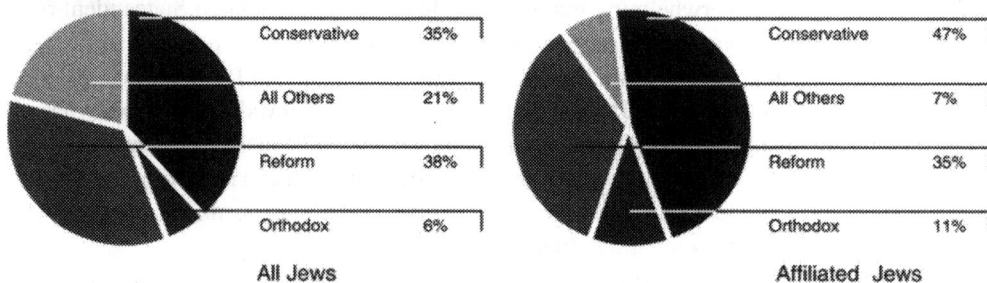

| Figure 1 | Distribution by Denomination of All Jews and Affiliated Jews |

All Jews

Conservative	35%
All Others	21%
Reform	38%
Orthodox	6%

Affiliated Jews

Conservative	47%
All Others	7%
Reform	35%
Orthodox	11%

in Rhode Island and South Broward (47 percent and 39 percent, respectively) — the two communities with the oldest age profiles — while they represent percentages well below those of the national average and other places in San Francisco and Seattle (at 20 percent each) (Table B). These western cities include a higher-than-average percentage of persons identified as Just Jewish or Other. Like Columbus and Dallas, they also have a high percentage who identify as Reform. The percentage identifying as Orthodox also ranges considerably, with a notably high percentage in New York and Columbus (13-14 percent) and very low percentages in Dallas and San Francisco (3-4 percent).

Jewish Identity of Conservative Jews
Even within denominations, heterogeneity exists. NJPS-1990 classified the Jewish population as Jews by religion (those who said they were Jewish when asked their religion in the screener question), as secular Jews (those reporting no religion but who considered themselves Jewish), and as Jews by choice (born as non-Jews but identifying as Jews in the survey, with or without conversion). Jews by religion were much more likely to identify with a specific denomination than were secular Jews; Jews by choice closely resembled Jews by religion.

While most of those professing a denominational identity reported themselves as Jews by religion, some secular Jews, and even some of the currently non-Jewish respondents (not included in this analysis), indicated that they identified with one of the four major denominations. Whether they were responding in terms of family identity, sympathy with a particular outlook, the denomination in which they were raised, or on some other basis cannot be ascertained. That they did so indicates the complexity of categorizing Jews. The denominational profiles that follow refer only to those who identified themselves as Jewish at the time of the survey.

Among Conservative Jews, the large majority (91 percent) identified as Jews by religion (Table 2). Nonetheless, some variation by age exists. While 90 percent or more in each age group are either a Jew by religion or a Jew by choice, the proportion reported as secular Jews rises from just over 3 percent of those aged 45 and over to over 9 percent of those aged 18-24. More younger Jews within the Conservative movement apparently regard their affiliation as having a cultural, ethnic, or historical content rather than primarily a religious one. This may help to explain the growing alienation of some Conservative Jews from religious/ritual observances even while they continue to identify as Conservative.

Viewed from a different perspective, seven-in-ten secular Conservative Jews are under age 45, compared to only 46 percent of the Conservative Jews by religion. This suggests that important changes may be occurring among Conservative Jews. Whether some of the younger secular Jews will change their self-identity as they grow older and progress further into the family cycle needs long-term follow-up. For the present, programming for Conservative Jews must take these differences into account.

Household Denominational Identification and Affiliation
NJPS-1990 ascertained denominational affiliation from several perspectives. In addition to the respondent's self-ascribed denomination, (s)he was also asked (1) the denomination of the household and (2) the denomination of anyone in the household who was affiliated with a synagogue/temple. The question on affiliation did not measure individual membership.

Of all the Jews, 35 percent were members of households with some affiliation, although it was not necessarily the denomination with which the respondent personally identified. Households with Conservative affiliations were the most prevalent, accounting for almost half of all synagogue/temple memberships (Figure 1). The Reform constituted just over one-third of the total, and the Orthodox almost 11 percent. Reconstructionists made up only 2 percent of all households, outnumbered by the 5 percent that did not identify with a particular denomination.

Households that were unaffiliated, but still identified with a particular denomination, were most likely to be Reform, followed by Conservative households. Very few were Orthodox, and even fewer were Reconstructionist. Because the denominations are distributed differently by whether or not the households are affiliated, the denominations vary in their specific levels of synagogue membership. Almost two-thirds of all Orthodox respondents reported that their

7

households were affiliated, but just under half of the Conservative and only one-third of the Reform respondents did so. The small groups of Reconstructionist respondents affiliated at a higher-than-average rate, 51 percent. Consistent with expectation, the lowest affiliation rates characterized those reporting themselves as Just Jewish or Other.

Whether the unaffiliated once held synagogue/temple membership may be of concern to those interested in raising membership rates or retaining current members. Of the 53 percent of Conservative Jews who were not members of affiliated households, one-third had been members at some earlier date (data not in table). The data do not identify when or why membership was terminated. They do suggest, however, that considerable attrition occurs and that synagogue membership might be higher if the reasons for these drop-outs were better understood and efforts made to counteract them.

The communities included in our study report Conservative membership in synagogues somewhat above the national average of 46 percent. The community levels have a comparatively wide range — from three-fourths or higher in Rhode Island and Columbus to the fifty-percent range in places as diverse as New York City, South Broward, San Francisco, and Seattle. Apparently, factors beyond community size, regional location, or even age of the Conservative population help to determine levels of membership. Some of the deviation from the national average may also be the result of differences in coverage and definitions used by the individual community surveys.

A high degree of congruity characterizes the denominational identity of individuals and the denominational affiliation of their household (Table 3). Among Conservative Jews, 83 percent lived in households that were affiliated with a Conservative synagogue. Of the balance, some 3 percent were affiliated with an Orthodox synagogue and 9 percent with a Reform temple. The Orthodox and Reform Jews display slightly more consistency; almost nine in ten reported their household belonged to a synagogue/temple of the same denomination. Virtually all of the Orthodox Jews whose households did not belong to an Orthodox synagogue were affiliated with a Conservative one, but the Reform respondents were somewhat more broadly distributed.

Overall, therefore, self-identity and household denominational affiliation are highly correlated. Whether self-identity accounts for the choice of affiliation or affiliation leads individuals to identify themselves with that denomination cannot be answered with the NJPS-1990 data.

Our ensuing analysis focuses on the characteristics of individuals, especially those of persons who identify themselves as Conservative Jews. In doing so, we often take account of synagogue/temple membership, recognizing that such affiliation refers to the household and not the individual. We are, therefore, referring to the general context within which the respondent is operating, rather than to membership of a specific individual.

Age Composition

For purposes of assessing age composition, we examine the entire Jewish population, adults and children.[2]   Conservative Jews are older on average than any other denominational group; their median age of 40.1 years is five years higher than that of either Orthodox or Reform Jews (Table 4), but the explanations for the variations differ. Fully one-fourth of Conservative Jews are elderly, almost as many as the Orthodox; both percentages are far higher than for the Jewish population as a whole. By contrast, only about half as many Reform Jews are elderly. Compared to the Orthodox, the Conservative population includes a much lower proportion of children; only one in five are under age 18 compared to almost one-third of the Orthodox, largely a result of the higher Orthodox fertility. Even the Reform Jews encompass a slightly higher percent under age 18 than do Conservative Jews, mirroring the high proportion of the Reform population concentrated in the reproductive years, aged 25-44, rather than a higher fertility rate. Only one-third of the Conservative Jews were at this stage of the life cycle.   That still fewer Orthodox Jews were in the 25-44 age group clearly points to higher fertility as the reason for the greater proportion of children among them.

These different profiles reflect the quite different histories of the various denominations as well as their current appeal to persons of different ages. That the elderly, who are generally more traditional in their religious orientation, form the largest segment of the Orthodox comes as no surprise. More surprising is the heavy concentration of older persons among the Conservatives.

The paucity of young persons in Conservative households suggests that future growth, in the absence of switching from other denominations, may be restricted. The generally heavier concentration of Reform and Reconstructionist Jews in the 25-44 age group and the larger reservoir of children in their households puts them in a better position for maintaining numerical strength over the next several decades.

The Just Jewish group closely resembles Reform Jews in its median age and in the comparatively low proportion of elderly and relatively high proportion of children. If a substantial number of

---

2. The denominational identification of children, that is, those under age 18, is based on the denominational identity of their household since information on current individual identity was obtained only for adult respondents.

persons in this "neutral" group opt for greater religious identity, they may provide recruits for the denominations. But in view of past trends involving shifts from more to less traditional affiliations, the Just Jewish group may grow, especially at the expense of key age cohorts among the denominations. The Other category is the youngest, with a median age of only 30 and an elderly population of only 5 percent; as many as four in ten are in the key 25-44 age group. Moreover, 30 percent of this group are under age 18. This age profile suggests that identifying as Other is a recent development, possibly the result of departures from the major denominations by younger persons in conjunction with mixed marriages. Later analysis of switching patterns will examine the effect of denominational change on the age structure of the various denominations.

Reflecting the differences in age patterns among the various denominations, the denominational composition of different segments of the age hierarchy also differs markedly. Conservative Jews account for almost half of all elderly Jews in the United States, even though the former are only one-third of the total Jewish population. The Conservative Jews thus constitute a far higher percentage of elderly Jews than of any other age group. Similarly, Orthodox Jews also account for a disproportional share of all Jewish elderly (10 percent) compared to the total proportion of Orthodox Jews in the total Jewish population. The preponderance of Conservative and Orthodox Jews in this oldest group reflects the concentration of immigrants and the second generation in the more traditional denominations. Conversely, the Conservatives are underrepresented among Jews aged 25-44 and even more so among those under age 18.

These age patterns among the Orthodox, Conservative, and Reform populations point to a major realignment in denominational affiliation as the composition of the Jewish community moves from the older, more heavily immigrant and second generation cohorts to younger American-born Jews. Still, since Conservative and Orthodox Jews have higher percentages in the 18-24 age group than in the 25-44 age group, the pattern of affiliation may be altering again, this time in the direction of more traditional denominations.

The possibility of shifts toward more traditional denominational identity among the young adults must, however, be seen in a broader context: Overall, more younger persons have opted to be secular or nondenominational rather than identify with a particular group. Whereas 13 percent of those aged 65 and older reported being Just Jewish or Other, this proportion rises consistently with declining age to one in five of those aged 25-44 and almost one-third of those aged 18-24. This suggests that the higher proportion of young adults reported as Conservative or Orthodox is not the result of net shifts from the secular Jewish population.

As earlier discussion has suggested, the age profiles of Conservative Jews in specific communities vary, although, among the eight communities included in our analysis, only two stand out as exceptional: South Broward and Rhode Island have unusually high percentages of elderly. South Broward's large population of Jews who are 65 and over is clearly due to the in-migration of retirees; Rhode Island's large percentage of elderly (36 percent) has resulted from the out-migration of younger persons, with very little in-migration to replace them. The other communities' elderly constitute between 16 percent and 23 percent of the adult population. Only Dallas stands out as having an unusually high percentage of young adults — 60 percent.

Among adult Conservative Jews, those who are members of affiliated households tend to be somewhat more concentrated in the two older age groups (Figure 2). Almost one-third are elderly, and another one-quarter are aged 45-64. By contrast, only one-quarter of the nonmembers are 65 and over, and just over one-fifth are 45-64. The younger age composition of the nonmembers is evident in the 45 percent who are aged 25-44, compared to only one-third of the affiliated who are in this group. With affiliation rates among Conservative Jews below 50 percent, the large proportion of younger adults living in unaffiliated households poses a potential threat to the strength of Conservative Jewry in the future. If they cannot be persuaded to join a congregation, the levels of affiliation may drop even further.

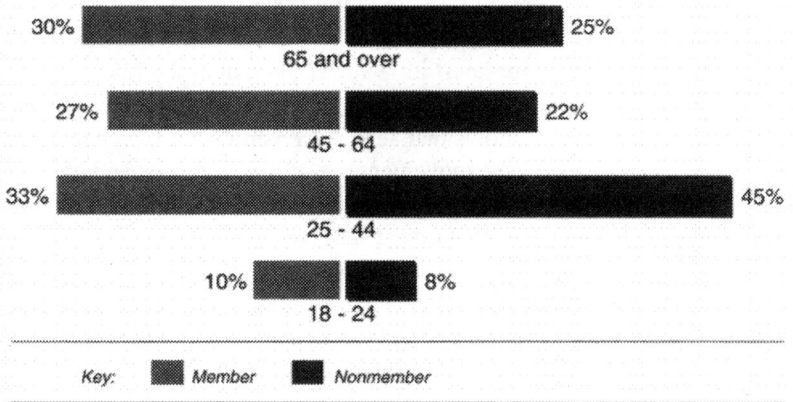

Figure 2 Age Profile of Adult Conservative Jews, Members and Nonmembers

30% 65 and over 25%
27% 45 - 64 22%
33% 25 - 44 45%
10% 18 - 24 8%

Key: Member Nonmember

An examination of the rates of past affiliation by age suggests that "disaffiliation" from synagogues is a cumulative process over the life cycle. From the 12 percent of the nonmember Conservative respondents aged 18-24 who reported a previous affiliation, the percent rises steadily to just over half (55 percent) of the elderly.

Regional Distribution

Reflecting both historical and recent economic forces that have made one or another region more attractive to Jews immigrating to the United States as well as to those migrating within the country, Orthodox, Conservative, Reform, Reconstructionist Jews, and those Just Jewish are not uniformly distributed among the major regions of the United States.

In 1900, two decades after the onset of massive Jewish immigration, 57 percent of American Jewry was concentrated in the Northeast region of the country, where the major ports of entry and their nearby areas were particularly attractive to immigrants. Another one-quarter lived in the Midwest, concentrated in such locations as Chicago, Detroit, and Cleveland. Only one-in-five Jews lived in the South or the West. The continued heavy influx of immigrants over the next several decades increased the concentration in the Northeast; by 1930, 68 percent of America's Jews were living in the region. The proportion in each of the other regions declined. Proportionally fewer lived in the Midwest (20 percent), and the South and West combined accounted for only 12 percent.

By the 1950s, the great reduction in immigration and the growing importance of internal migration led to a substantial redistribution of the Jewish population among regions, as was true of the American population as a whole. The proportion of Jews residing in the Northeast declined continuously, while sharp rises occurred in the proportion living in the West and, to a lesser extent, in the South. NJPS-1990 ascertained that only 46 percent of Jewish Americans lived in the Northeast in 1990, 11 percent in the Midwest, 22 percent in the South, and 21 percent in the West. This major realignment among the regions shows that Jews have participated, perhaps in accentuated form, in the movement out of the Northeast and Midwest to the South and West, which has characterized the American population generally (cf. Long, 1988).

While Jews remain heavily concentrated in the Northeast, the changing distribution suggests that Jews, feeling increasingly accepted in America, are paralleling mainstream America in shifting to the Sunbelt regions of the country. Economic and quality-of-life factors associated with both employment and retirement have played important roles in this redistribution. Previously, more weight was probably given to concerns about being close to family and to concentrations of Jewish population and their institutional facilities and religious amenities. Particularly as the denominational composition of the Jewish population changed and as adherence to traditional practices weakened, so, too, Jews gave lower priority to living in areas of heavy Jewish concentration. If so, one would expect the Orthodox and, to a lesser extent, Conservative Jews to remain more concentrated in the Northeast, and the Reform, Reconstructionist, and Just Jewish populations to be located more heavily in other regions.

Differences in regional distribution cannot be ascribed entirely or even mainly to the effects of selective migration. They may also stem from differences in the historical development of various Jewish communities, to variations in socioeconomic and denominational composition, to the size of the individual communities in the varied regions, and to variations across regions in attitudes toward Jews and in Jewish attitudes and practices vis a vis intermarriage, ritual observance, and Jewish education.

Given these considerations, not surprisingly, our data show the Northeast to have a heavy concentration of those with a more traditional orientation (Table 6). Fully 70 percent of adult Orthodox Jews lived in this region, compared to only 45 percent of the Conservative, 41 percent of the Reform, and still fewer of the Reconstructionist Jews. As many as half of the Just Jewish also lived in the Northeast. By contrast, the South and the West each contained only 11 percent of the Orthodox population, but almost one-fifth to one-fourth of the Conservative and Reform Jews. The Midwest, having declined in importance as an area of Jewish settlement, included between 8 and 12 percent of each of the three major denominational groups.

Relatively more of the small number of Reconstructionist Jews lived in the West (25 percent) and in the Midwest (21 percent) than was the case for the three major denominations. Consistent with expectation, the Just Jewish had comparatively more adherents living in the West (29 percent); like the Orthodox, relatively few lived in the Midwest and South. This bipolar distribution may reflect the more cosmopolitan environment of the major metropolitan areas in the two coastal regions.

The distribution of Conservative Jews among the regions of the country varies considerably by age, partly related to different patterns of migration and population redistribution. Compared to any older age group, fewer of those aged 18-44 lived in the Northeast; and considerably more resided in the West. By contrast, more than half of the middle-age group resided in the Northeast; and, compared to both older and younger age groups, fewer lived in the South or West. Not surprisingly, because of retirement migration, the elderly were more heavily concentrated in the South — almost one-third — and had the

Figure 3	Regional Distribution of Adult Conservative Jews, Members and Nonmembers

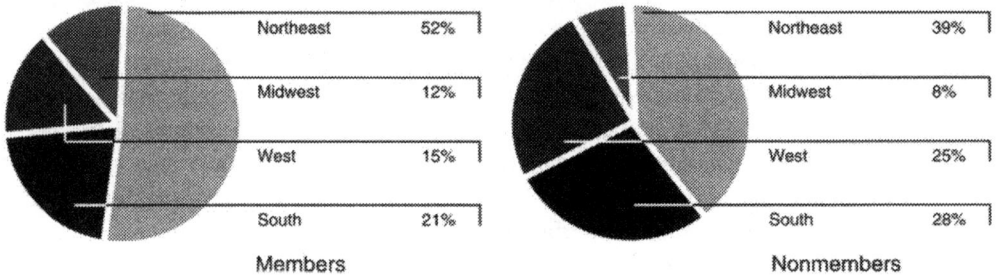

Northeast	52%
Midwest	12%
West	15%
South	21%

Members

Northeast	39%
Midwest	8%
West	25%
South	28%

Nonmembers

lowest proportion living in the Midwest.

When we distinguish between Conservative Jews who are members of households affiliated with synagogues and temples and those who are not, more of those in affiliated households (52 percent) are located in the Northeast and fewer in the West (Figure 3). Fewer members are also in the South. Generally, these regional differences in the rates of synagogue affiliation conform to what might be expected when we take into account the intensity of Jewish life in the different regions.

Moreover, synagogue membership levels of Conservative Jews vary significantly by region of residence (data not in tables). In the Northeast, just over half of the respondents reported that they or another member of their household belonged to a synagogue, and almost as many (48 percent) in the Midwest were affiliated. In the South and the West, however, membership levels were much lower, only about one-third.

Metropolitan Residence

The Jewish population has not only participated in national patterns of mobility but also moved within metropolitan areas. Large numbers have shifted from the cities to the suburbs and sometimes to outlying parts of metropolitan areas and even into small towns outside metropolitan areas (Goldstein, 1992; Goldstein and Goldstein, 1996). Again, the question is whether this redistribution is also connected to denominational preferences.

Historically, Jews were concentrated in the major cities of the United States, partly for religious reasons — their religious practices required easy access to synagogues, religious schools, kosher butchers, and mikvehs — and partly for social and economic reasons. As their socioeconomic status rose, they left the ghetto areas for better sections of the cities and eventually for the suburbs. The latter movement was facilitated by weakened adherence to halakhah, so that fewer Jews needed easy access to religious institutions. Over time, the dispersal became so great that travel over considerable distances would have been required to maintain institutional connections; for many, the ties weakened either as the cause or effect of greater assimilation.

To the extent that observance of halakhah varies among the members of the different denominations, we would expect, other things being equal, that the most observant (Orthodox) will be most concentrated in urban centers while more of those with lower levels of observance, the Reform and the Just Jewish, will be located in the outlying parts of metropolitan areas or even outside them. We would expect Conservative Jews to be intermediate.

The data support this thesis, although the extent of difference between Conservative and Reform Jews is not as sharp as expected (Table 7). In 1990, just over half of self-identified Conservative Jews lived in the central cities of metropolitan areas, as did the Reform, Reconstructionist, and Just Jewish populations. By contrast, almost three-fourths of Orthodox Jews lived in the central cities. Apparently, the underlying process of redistribution has been virtually the same for all groups but the Orthodox. The practices and religious needs of the latter lead to continued high rates of residence in urban centers, even while their areas of concentration within the cities may change as a result of the ecological succession of various ethnic/racial groups.

Clearly, all of the non-Orthodox groups have participated in the movement to suburbia: Between 21 and 26 percent live outside the central city but in the same county as that in which it is located; only 9 percent of the Orthodox do so. About 15 percent of Conservative and Reform Jews have located in suburban counties beyond the central city, and as many as 11 percent live even outside such limits and in nonmetropolitan areas. By contrast, fewer of the Just Jewish live in the suburban counties, and more reside beyond the suburbs (16 percent); this pattern is consistent with their generally low level of traditional observance. That Conservative Jews differ minimally from Reform Jews suggests that residential amenities and housing factors play a similar role in decisions on where to locate. Proximity to religious institutions and the Jewish composition of neighborhood are of lower priority than among the Orthodox.

The residential distribution of Conservative Jews differed considerably by age group. While persons of all ages were more likely to live in central cities than elsewhere, the percentage was lowest for the young and highest for the elderly. Minimal age differences characterized the proportions living in the immediate suburbs, but more distant suburban residence was inversely related to age. Almost one in five of the young compared to only half as many of the aged lived in suburban counties. Moreover, relatively more of the young and the middle-aged than of the elderly lived in areas even further removed from the central city. Younger segments of the Conservative population clearly have a more dispersed residential pattern — which adds to the challenge of integrating them into the organized life of the community.

Interestingly, relatively more Conservative synagogue members live in the suburban and more outlying parts of metropolitan areas than do nonmembers. This may be due to the movement of synagogues from central cities to suburbs, the way in which membership requirements and participation are linked, and the different age and life cycle profiles of the residents of the various segments of metropolitan areas. The relatively high percentage of nonmembers living in nonmetropolitan areas is not surprising; it relates in part to the absence of synagogues in smaller towns and rural locations and partly to the lower interest that Jews living in such areas have in synagogue involvement. For example, only 15 percent of the nonmember Conservative Jews living outside metropolitan areas had ever belonged to a synagogue (data not in table). This contrasted with one-third or more of the nonmembers living inside the metropolitan area.

* * * * *

Our analysis thus shows distinct denominational differences among Jewish Americans in basic distinguishing characteristics like age and regional distribution. Especially notable is the higher average age of Conservative Jews when compared to Orthodox, Reform, or Reconstructionist Jews. We have further noted the relevance of whether or not persons who self-identify as Conservative Jews are synagogue members. Even the relative size of the major movements changes when affiliation is taken into account; because Conservative Judaism has higher affiliation levels than the Reform movement, Conservative Jewry constitutes the highest percentage of all affiliated Jews although, in general, more persons identify as Reform Jews. The importance of membership and age in accounting for differences in characteristics among Conservative Jews and between Conservative Jews and persons identified with other denominations or the nondenominational will be a dominant theme in the discussions that follow.

III. Social and Demographic Profile

Examination of a range of socioeconomic characteristics indicates that Conservative Jews are intermediate in their profiles between the Orthodox and Reform populations. Recognizing what these characteristics are and assessing how Conservative Jews differ from those identifying with other denominations or with no denomination is a key to understanding the current demographic situation and its implications for the future of Conservative Jewry.

Generation Status

Together with age, generation status is a major demographic background variable distinguishing those identifying with the various denominations in the United States. The changing generation status of the Jewish American population has great importance for its future. Since the imposition of the quota laws in the 1920s, Jews who are third generation and higher have had no massive reinforcement from immigrant flows from strong overseas Jewish communities. Because of the relatively small numbers of Holocaust refugees and the often weak Jewish identity of the recent Soviet immigrants, these refugee flows have not significantly altered either the overall demographic composition of American Jewry or its socioreligious profile. The impact on selected localities where recent immigrants are concentrated may be stronger.

The changing generational profile of American Jews is indicative of their growing distance from the immigrant experience and the traditional attitudes and practices that were characteristic of the immigrant generation. By 1990, the percentage of foreign-born in the Jewish population had declined to only 9 percent. Many were elderly, directly reflecting the changing pattern of Jewish immigration to the United States; 17 percent of the population aged 65 and over were foreign-born, contrasted to only 4 percent of those under age 18. Similarly, increasing numbers of Jewish Americans are now descended not only from American-born parents but also from American-born grandparents.

Among Conservative Jews, 9 percent reported no foreign-born grandparents, while 69 percent had all foreign-born grandparents (Table 8). In fact, 10 percent (not shown) were themselves foreign born. The generational status of Conservative Jews is intermediate between the Orthodox (who had a higher percentage of all foreign-born) and Reform Jews (more of whose grandparents were all born in the United States). Those who identified as Just Jewish and, especially, those classified as Other had the highest percentages of all

native-born grandparents. Not surprisingly, distance from the
immigrant generation varies inversely with age.

Patterns of synagogue membership among Conservative Jews
are also related to immigrant ties: Synagogue members were more
likely to have four foreign-born grandparents than were nonmembers.
This means that members were closer to their immigrant roots than
were nonmembers. As documented by other studies (e.g., Goldstein
and Goldscheider, 1968), the generation status of the Jewish
population is closely related to indicators of more traditional
religious behavior.

The patterns, of course, vary from one community to another.
South Broward, not surprisingly, has an exceptionally high percentage
(93 percent) of its population reporting four foreign-born grandparents.
More striking is the very low percentage reported for Columbus: Only
43 percent of its population have four grandparents born abroad, while
15 percent are at least third generation. The early settlement of Jews
in the Midwest and the relatively smaller influx of foreign-born in the
twentieth century may explain the difference.

As the elderly population dies, increasing proportions of
Conservative Jewry will have no direct memory of their immigrant
forebears. The infusion of Yiddishkeit (whether in religious or ethnic
form), which has often been provided by grandparents, will cease to be
a major factor in the identity of Conservative Jews, as it will be for
Jewish Americans generally. A much greater burden is thus placed on
the community to fill this important role.

Life-Cycle Status

Changes in age composition and life-style have resulted in changing
living arrangements for the American population as a whole, as well as
for Jews. There are more elderly people, many of whom are widowed,
and more adult children who leave their parental homes, some to
return later. More couples cohabit without formal marriage; and
finally, there are increased rates of divorce and single parenthood. All
have contributed to changing the composition of the household unit.
To the extent that religious activities are heavily focused on the family
as a unit, the nature of the household unit becomes an important
feature of the population. The information available in NJPS-1990
was used to ascertain the type of household of which each respondent
was a member. We can, thereby, compare Conservative households,
classified on the basis of the denominational identity of the respondent,
with those of other denominations.

The denominations differ in their household composition,
reflecting a complex set of factors: differences in age composition, age
at marriage, the proportion who marry, the level and timing of

childbearing, the extent of divorce, and the proportion of elderly who are widowed (Table 9). Some 27 percent of Conservative households consist of one-person units (Figure 4). This percentage is below that of Orthodox Jews and quite similar to that of Reform Jews. For all three denominations, but especially for the Orthodox one, a majority of the one-person units are aged 45 and over.

Figure 4 **Distribution by Life-Cycle Stage of Conservative Jews**

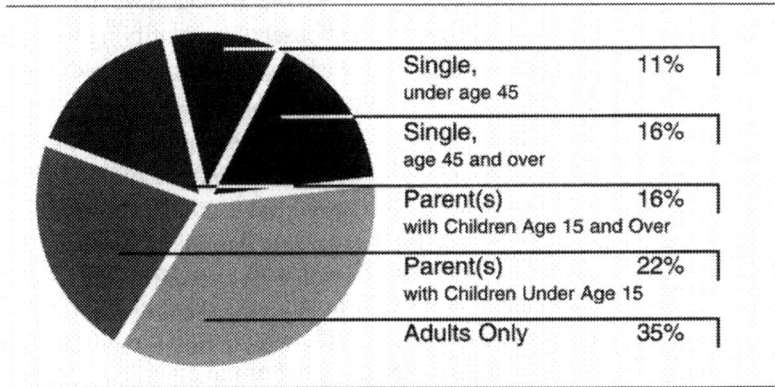

Single, under age 45	11%
Single, age 45 and over	16%
Parent(s) with Children Age 15 and Over	16%
Parent(s) with Children Under Age 15	22%
Adults Only	35%

Conservative and Reform Jews closely resemble each other in their proportion of units with two or more adults only. For both, just over one-third of all households fall in this category, whereas among Orthodox Jews, only 29 percent do the latter, reflecting the higher percentage of units that have already been broken by the death of a spouse. Notably, among all groups, over half of all units have no children living at home. This has obvious importance for programming and planning activities. We can no longer assume that the large majority of Conservative Jews are in traditional families, consisting of parents with children under age 18. Instead, membership in synagogues and involvement in activities must also cater to the interests of childless households, many of which consist of persons living alone.

About four-in-ten units in each of the three major denominations consist of one or both parents living with children, but they are differentially distributed between those containing young children (under age 15) and those including only children aged 15 and over (some older children may be in the units containing younger children). Conservative households have the lowest proportion with younger children at home, 22 percent of all units. Among the Orthodox and Reform households, the comparable proportion is 29 percent. This pattern again points to the importance of taking family

composition into account in programming and other planning
decisions. With less than one-quarter of all Conservative units
containing children under age 15, attention clearly must also be given
to families at other stages of the life cycle. The relatively small
percent of these younger families limits the extent to which the
Conservative movement can rely on its own younger population for
future maintenance of size and, even more so, for growth; this situation
highlights the need both to retain the young adult pool of Conservative
Jews and to recruit new members from among those not identified with
a denomination as well as from among those in other denominations.

In contrast to the households identifying with the three major
denominations, Just Jewish and Other households have lower
proportions of one-person units. Particularly striking is the
Reconstructionist pattern: A disproportionate number are in younger
one-persons households and in adults-only households. Among those
with children, the large majority have children under age 15 in their
households. This pattern is largely due to the younger age
composition of the Reconstructionist population. It points, however, to
their potential for growth as the younger children mature and as
couples begin to have children. This likely future growth stands in
sharp contrast to the potential of the other major denominations and
may be particularly serious for the Conservative movement since, as
later analysis will document, many of the persons currently identified
as Reconstructionist were raised as Conservative.

Not surprisingly, among Conservative Jews the household
composition of synagogue members and nonmembers differs
markedly. Members have a much higher percentage of households
consisting of parent(s) with children (45 percent) than do nonmembers
(31 percent). Clearly, children in the household are a key to whether a
family joins, or leaves, a synagogue. Among parents with children, a
disproportionate number of the nonmembers have children under age
15. Relatively more nonmembers are in adults-only units or in single-
person units. Interestingly, within the one-person units, far more of
those belonging to a synagogue are aged 45 and over; whereas, among
the nonmembers, one-person units are almost equally divided between
younger and older persons.

Changing household composition also affects whether a
household drops synagogue affiliation. Only one in five nonmembers
with children under age 15 reported a former membership. By
contrast, relatively twice as many nonmembers with children aged 15
and over had held synagogue membership in the past. A sharp
difference also characterized the two categories of single-person units.
Conservative nonmembers aged 45 and over were twice as likely to
have formerly belonged than those who were under age 45. Thus,

fewer younger single persons were currently members and fewer of those who did not belong had been affiliated earlier. This group, therefore, provides an untapped reservoir of potential members.

The stages of the life cycle and the age of respondent are clearly related to each other. Conservative respondents under age 45 are concentrated either in single or adults-only units, or in households with young children. Middle-aged respondents are most like to be either in adults-only units — because, for many, children had already left home — or in households with older children only. By contrast, the elderly are almost entirely in one-person or adults-only households.

Marital Status

Marriage and the family are basic to Judaism, playing a key role for the future through reproduction and their function as the major agents of socialization and the transmission of values, attitudes, goals, and aspirations. Whether current adult members of the community identify as Orthodox, Conservative, or Reform is, to a considerable degree, influenced by the denominational identity of their parents and the households in which they were raised. Attention to the marital status, intermarriage patterns, and childbearing of Conservative Jews in 1990 is, therefore, an essential part of any evaluation of their current demographic situation and their future strength in America.

For the adult Jewish population as a whole, almost six in ten were married at the time of the 1990 survey. Reflecting their older age at marriage, 26 percent of the men were still single compared to only 18 percent of women. By contrast, because they live longer on average, women are more likely than men to be widowed. Overall, men and women in the different denominational groups closely resembled each other in the proportion currently married, although the pattern is somewhat more variable for women. Notable is the much higher percentage of separated/divorced among Conservative and Reform women than among either Orthodox women or men of any denomination. The latter differential reflects the higher remarriage rate of men.

Among Conservative Jews, consistently more of those affiliated with synagogues were married, probably due to the role of marriage and family in stimulating higher affiliation rates. Conversely, especially among men, more of the nonmembers had never been married. Sharp differences also characterize the proportion of members and nonmembers who were divorced/separated, with far more divorced/separated among the nonmembers. Overall, these patterns suggest that Conservative singles and divorced/separated nonmembers may constitute a pool of potential synagogue members, even while the married nonmembers can also serve as an important source of membership.

Marital status is highly correlated with age and sex. Among the youngest group of Conservative adults, both men and women reflect the older age of marriage common among Jews; only half of the women and only slightly fewer men in this age group are married, and, conversely, the percentage of singles is very high. In fact, an examination of more detailed age data indicates that, among Conservative men, about two-thirds had not yet married by age 30; by age 40 this was true of only one-quarter, still a high proportion compared to the pattern in the general population. The earlier age at marriage of women is evidenced in the lower proportion still single by age 30 — only one-third; but, like men, one-quarter of Conservative women aged 40 had not yet married. Late marriage and possibly no marriage at all seems to have become a common feature of younger Conservative Jews.

Also noteworthy, 11 percent of the men and 12 percent of the women aged 18-44 were separated or divorced at the time of the survey. Among the middle-aged, one-in-five women were separated or divorced. That the level is very much lower for men (only 9 percent) indicates the greater ease with which men remarry after a divorce. The relative ease of male remarriage and the greater longevity of women are reflected in the oldest age group, among whom four times as many women as men are widowed. The relatively high levels of divorce/separation among Conservative Jews, especially among the younger ones, suggest that the traditional family configuration, which depends on a married couple at its core, is in danger. The implications for the transmission of Conservative values and the orientation of programming, which is usually geared to in-tact families, will need serious reconsideration.

Because marital status, and particularly widowhood, is so closely related to age, variations in the marital status distribution of Conservative Jews in the various communities reflect their age structures. Thus, South Broward has an exceptionally high percentage of widowed (35 percent), whereas Columbus, Dallas, and San Francisco — relatively young Jewish communities — have higher-than-average percentages of those never married (about one in five). That Boston and New York also have such high proportions of singles most likely relates to the educational and career opportunities that are specific to these locations.

Intermarriage

Without doubt, the most startling statistic to emerge from NJPS-1990 was the high rate of intermarriage that had come to characterize the Jewish population. NJPS 1970-71 found that 8 percent of all married

Jews were married to non-Jews; the 1990 survey identified 28 percent of all married Jews in mixed marriages. Even more striking was the evidence from NJPS-1990 that the percent of mixed marriages rose from 9 percent of those married prior to 1965 to 52 percent of those married in the five years before the survey.

We expect the rates of intermarriage to vary by denomination, given differences in commitment to halakhah and changes in policy among the Reform, allowing patrilineal as well as matrilineal descent; only matrilineal descent is recognized by the Conservative and Orthodox movements. The data support our expectation. In the discussion that follows, denominational identification refers to that of the respondent, i.e., the Jewish partner in mixed marriages. Since we cannot account for respondents who switched their denomination because of intermarriage, the levels for Conservative Jews, as for others, may be an underestimate.

Consistent with their centrist position on the religio-traditional continuum, Conservatives Jews had levels of mixed marriages (21 percent) that were intermediary between Orthodox (7 percent) and Reform (38 percent) (Table 11).[3] The level of mixed marriages for Reconstructionist Jews was higher than that for Reform Jews; it was even higher for the Just Jewish and the Other groups. Only small percentages in any denomination reported being "Jews by Choice".[4] Only 8 percent of all marriages among Conservatives and 3 percent among Orthodox involved the assumption of a Jewish identity by the spouse who was not born Jewish; for the Reform, the proportion was 10 percent. The low rates of conversion, even under the broad criteria employed, point to the significant change that has characterized marriage patterns. Not only are more Jews marrying persons not born

3. Intermarriage is defined here as follows for the *core Jewish population:*

For respondents who indicated that they were born Jewish or that religion at birth was None: (a) if spouse was born Jewish, marriage status equals in-marriage; (b) if spouse was born non-Jewish but is currently Jewish, marriage status equals conversionary; (c) if spouse was born non-Jewish and is currently non-Jewish, marriage status equals mixed.

For respondents who indicated they were born in some other religion but were currently Jewish: (a) if the spouse was born Jewish, marriage status equals conversionary; (b) if the spouse was not born Jewish but is currently Jewish, marriage status equals conversionary; (c)if the spouse was born non-Jewish and is currently non-Jewish, marriage status equals mixed.

Respondents who indicated their current religion was non-Jewish were not considered, since they would not have been defined as part of the core Jewish population.

4. NJPS-1990 asked no direct questions about formal conversion since there was no way to judge whether the conversion met halakhic standards. If persons not born Jewish were reported as Jewish at the time of the survey, they were classified as Jews by choice. Some persons in this category, therefore, did not undergo a formal conversion to Judaism.

Jewish, but in few of these marriages does the non-Jew choose to become Jewish.

This change is correlated with the generally greater acceptance of mixed marriages both in the larger society and in the Jewish community. According to NJPS-1990, when asked their attitude toward having their children marry a non-Jew, only 28 percent of the Conservative respondents reported they would oppose such a marriage (Table 12). This compared to 56 percent of the Orthodox but only 9 percent of the Reform. Indeed, about one-quarter of Conservative Jews indicated they would be supportive of such a marriage. Fewer of the Orthodox (14 percent), but far more of the Reform (40 percent), held such attitudes. The highest levels of support for children who choose to enter mixed marriages characterized Reconstructionist Jews and the Just Jewish.

Judged by the proportion of mixed marriages, Conservative Jews are over twice as likely as Orthodox Jews to be in such marriages, but only about half as frequently as Reform Jews, and even less frequently than the Reconstructionist Jews and Just Jewish. Nonetheless, with almost one-in-five marriages being mixed, Conservative Judaism clearly faces a major challenge. In developing guidelines for membership, for leadership roles, and for religious schools, the Conservative leadership must be able to reach out to the intermarried — especially the Jewish partner — even while emphasizing the importance of homogamous marriages. The line between outreach and strengthening the position of committed Conservative Jews is a fine one.

Not surprisingly, rates of mixed marriage differ sharply between those who are synagogue members and those who are not (Figure 5).

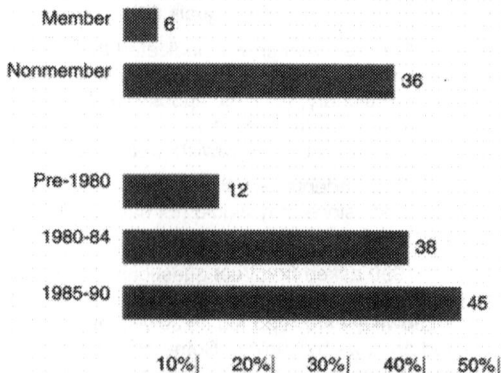

Figure 5   **Percent of Conservative Jews Who Are Intermarried by Marriage Cohort, and by Membership Status**

Category	Percent
Member	6
Nonmember	36
Pre-1980	12
1980-84	38
1985-90	45

10%   20%   30%   40%   50%

Among Conservative Jews, only 6 percent of synagogue members were in mixed marriages compared to 36 percent of the nonmembers. And paralleling the actual rates of mixed marriage, far more of those who were synagogue members reported they would oppose a mixed marriage than did the nonmembers; more of the nonmembers reported they would be supportive. To the extent that membership reflects a stronger identification with Judaism, the higher rates of mixed marriage among nonmembers may stem from weaker identity. On the other hand, entering a mixed marriage may also lead individuals to weaken their Jewish identity and their ties to the organized community, especially if the community itself has barriers to participation of the Jewish spouse and, even more so, of the non-Jewish spouse in synagogue membership and activities.

This pattern extends to former members. Just over half of the in-married who were not current members formerly belonged to a synagogue, as did just over one-fourth of the smaller proportion of nonmembers among the conversionary marriages. However, none of those in mixed marriages who were nonmembers had, as adults, previously belonged to a synagogue.

These statistics suggest considerable alienation among the mixed married from organized religious life, both earlier and currently. Whether this attitude initially contributed to an intermarriage or whether the intermarried feel unwelcome in a synagogue, especially when the non-Jewish members of their family cannot fully participate, is not apparent from the data. Understanding the underlying motivations for this pattern is, however, essential if Conservative Judaism is to cope successfully with the high levels of mixed marriage among its adherents, and if it is to attract to Judaism the spouses and, especially, the children of such marriages. Such outreach would be important if the movement wants to maintain its numerical strength. High levels of mixed marriages and the subsequent loss to Judaism of most of the children of these marriages would result in decline in numbers unless the process of attrition is reversed.

Comparisons of rates of intermarriage among communities are difficult because of definitional differences employed by the surveys. Some surveys are based on lists of known Jews only, while others define intermarriage in restrictive fashion (e.g., Jews married to persons with no religion are not considered intermarried). Among communities that can be compared, Seattle, for example, reports intermarriage of persons identifying as Conservative Jews at 5 percent, but this excludes Jews married to persons without any religion (22 percent). Within these limitations, the levels of intermarriage vary from a low of 2 percent in South Broward to a high of 11 percent in Columbus. Local variations, like age and generation status, may, therefore, play a key role in decisions about the kinds of programming that may be desirable to reach the intermarried population.

That Conservative Jews have participated in the sharp increase in intermarriage is evidenced in the comparative data on rates of mixed marriages and conversions by marriage cohort. Only 12 percent of those Conservative Jews married before 1980 were married to a person not born Jewish, and 5 percent were in marriages in which the non-Jewish spouses had become Jews by choice. By contrast, among those married between 1980 and 1984, 38 percent were intermarried; another 15 percent were married to a spouse who had been born non-Jewish but who had chosen to identify as a Jew. The trend toward higher levels of intermarriage continued among those married in 1985-1990. The rate of mixed marriages rose to 45 percent; another 15 percent were in conversionary marriages

Clearly, Conservative Jewry is facing a major problem. A high proportion of younger self-identified Conservative Jews are intermarried, and few have chosen to create a more homogeneous religious environment through the identification of the non-Jewish partner with Judaism, either through formal conversion or by simply choosing to live as a Jew by choice. Perhaps most important is the significance this has for the children of such marriages. Many may not be halakhically Jewish if they were born to a non-Jewish mother, even if she has chosen to identify as a Jew rather than to formally convert. How such children will be incorporated into Judaism and the Conservative movement, possibly with eventual formal conversion, is an issue of pressing urgency

The rising levels of mixed marriages among younger marriage cohorts parallel the greater acceptance of mixed marriages among younger persons as measured by the percentage of respondents indicating support for such marriages (Table 12).[5] Among the elderly, 29 percent indicated they would oppose such marriages for their children, and only 19 percent said they would be supportive of such a marriage. Declining age was associated with increasing levels of supportiveness and generally a decrease in the proportion who would oppose such a marriage. For example, only 24 percent of those aged 25-44 reported they would oppose a mixed marriage, while 30 percent said they would be supportive. The changed trend among the 18-24 age group in the proportion opposing intermarriage is notable; a higher percent would oppose mixed marriages than was true of the 25-44 age group. At the same time, a higher percent of those aged 18-24 is also supportive (35 percent). Whether these younger persons will become even more accepting of intermarriage as their own children come

---

5. The percentage of respondents who indicated that they would accept or be neutral toward the mixed marriage of their children is omitted from the table.

closer to marriage age remains to be seen.

Most noteworthy, across all age groups, only a minority of Conservative Jews would be opposed to their children entering a mixed marriage. The substantial number who would be supportive, especially among younger groups, and the large number who were neutral point to the large-scale absence within the family itself of strong pressures against mixed marriages.

Not surprisingly, attitudes toward intermarriage are highly correlated with synagogue membership. Far more members (35 percent) than nonmembers (21 percent) were opposed to intermarriage. Obviously, involvement in organized religious life reflects and is affected by attitudes of Conservative Jews toward mixed marriage.

Education

Jewish Americans have compiled an extraordinary record of educational achievement. This reflects the great emphasis placed on education, both as an intrinsic value and as a means of social mobility. By 1990, three-fourths of the adult Jewish population aged 25 and over had some college education. As many as 53 percent had completed college, and half of these had undertaken graduate studies. Reflecting their different generation and age composition and possibly also their economic background, Conservative, Orthodox, and Reform Jews differed considerably in their educational profiles (Table 13).

Among Conservative Jews, one-fourth had a graduate education and almost another quarter had completed college. Only one-third had not had any college education. By comparison, the Orthodox were, on average, slightly less educated, and Reform Jews received the highest levels of education. Even more striking is the very high percentage of Reconstructionist Jews who had a college or graduate education -- fully 83 percent.

Consistently, members of Conservative synagogues had more education than nonmembers. For example, 55 percent of the members had completed college compared to only 42 percent of the nonmembers. Conversely, more of the nonmembers than members had a high school education or less. Whether the association of more education with higher rates of synagogue membership is a function of attitudes or ability to finance membership cannot be ascertained from the NJPS-1990 data. Among those who were nonmembers in 1990, the educational differences in former levels of membership are small.

Educational achievement varies widely across communities, reflecting both local age distributions and opportunity structures. In general, the Conservative populations of communities in the West have higher levels of education than those in the East. For example, whereas 30-39 percent of those living in Boston or Rhode Island had a

---

Figure 6   **Educational Achievements of Conservative Jews, by Age**

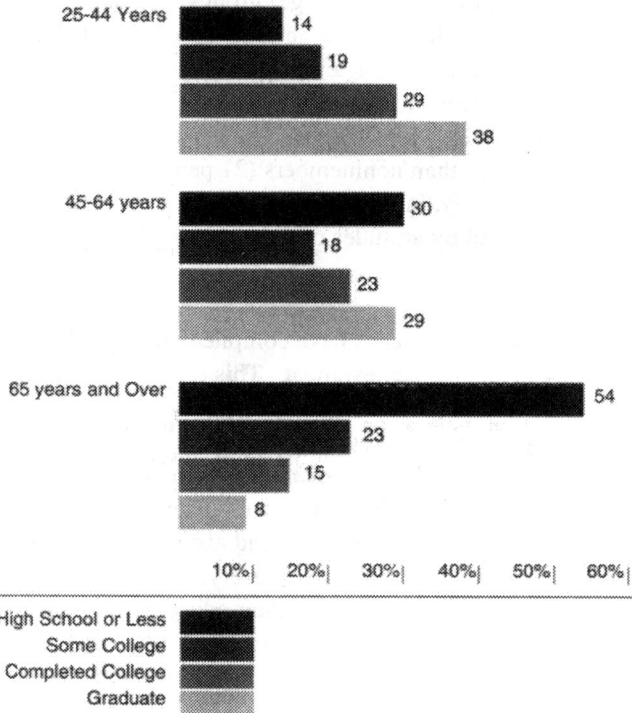

25-44 Years
- 14
- 19
- 29
- 38

45-64 years
- 30
- 18
- 23
- 29

65 years and Over
- 54
- 23
- 15
- 8

10% | 20% | 30% | 40% | 50% | 60% |

High School or Less
Some College
Completed College
Graduate

---

high school education or less, this was true of only 12-14 percent in the western cities. Conversely, generally higher percentages in western communities had postgraduate education, with the 57 percent postgraduates in Seattle outstandingly high.

For Conservative Jews, as for the Jewish population as a whole, the level of educational achievement also varies widely by age, reflecting temporal differentials in opportunities in the form of economic constraints and discrimination (Figure 6). Among the elderly, just over half had only a high school education or less, only 9 percent had received a graduate education, and over one-third had at least some college education but had not gone on to graduate studies. Among those aged 25-44, by contrast, only 14 percent had less than some college education, almost half had at least some college education, and as many as 38 percent had been enrolled in graduate studies. The variations by age point to the challenge that the community as a whole as well as the Conservative movement face in serving the needs and interests of a population that has become increasingly educated and sophisticated.

Labor Force Participation

Rates of labor force participation are closely linked to life-cycle stage, reflecting postponed entry into the labor force due to continuing education; marriage, childbearing, and child-rearing, especially on the part of women; and retirement patterns (Hartman and Hartman, 1996:61-114). Consistent with patterns in the general population, the proportion of Jewish men actively participating in the labor force in 1990 rose from 40 percent of those aged 18-24 to a peak of 94 percent in the prime working ages 35-44. At first gradually and then precipitously, the percent in the labor force declined to 26 percent of the elderly men. The overall pattern of age differentials for women closely parallels that of men, although women's labor force participation peaks earlier than men's, and the levels of participation are lower at all ages but the youngest, because women aged 18-24 are less likely than men to be still enrolled as students.

Rates of labor force participation vary substantially among the denominations, partly reflecting differences in their age structures and partly reflecting differences in the roles of women (Table 14). Over 70 percent of all Conservative men were in the labor force (including employed and unemployed) compared to only 54 percent of Orthodox men and 81 percent of Reform men. In large measure, the differences for men reflect the impact of age and the concomitant percentages who are retired. In each denomination, fewer women than men were working. Among Conservative women, 55 percent were in the labor force, compared to only 36 percent of the Orthodox women (far more were homemakers) and 62 percent of the Reform women.

Within the Conservative group, as in the general population, the different age cohorts vary considerably in labor force status. Among the youngest group of men, half were still students, but by age 30, virtually all Conservative men were in the labor force. Retirement began for some as early as age 45, and rose with increasing age, reaching seven in ten among those aged 65 and over. The elderly, thus, constitute a large reservoir of persons who may have the time and skills, and perhaps even the need, to become involved in community and synagogue activities. At the same time, they constitute a substantial sector of the Conservative population that may be operating with constrained financial resources.

Like men, the majority of younger Conservative women were students, but women's labor force participation peaked quite early — to almost nine in ten of those aged 25-29. Thereafter, through ages 30-39, a growing proportion were homemakers, as one-in-four women became involved in child-rearing. Reflecting a return to the labor force as children entered school, female labor force participation rates peaked again at ages 45-49. Thereafter, the proportion of homemakers rises sharply as does the percent of retired. By age 65 and over, only one-in-five elderly women were still in the labor force.

The patterns for women take on special significance because of their important roles in voluntary activities. Their high levels of labor force participation point to the changed demands on women's time and the constraints many feel about active involvement in voluntary and organizational activities. Institutions like synagogues may have to adjust their volunteer recruitment efforts to place greater reliance upon older, retired members of the community, many of whom have much-needed skills and experience.

The close relation of age and employment status is clearly apparent in community variations. Our two oldest communities, Rhode Island and South Broward, have exceptionally high proportions of retired and many fewer in the labor force. New York is also exceptional in having a relatively small percentage (64 percent) in the labor force and larger-than-average proportions reported as homemakers and other; its 9 percent retired is unusually low.

Occupational Composition

The high occupational achievement of Jews parallels their distinctive educational record (Goldstein, 1992; Hartman and Hartman, 1996). Community studies in every decade since the 1950s, as well as NJPS-1970/71 and NJPS-1990, have shown Jews as heavily concentrated in the upper ranks of the occupational hierarchy, much more so than the white population of the United States. Within the white-collar group, the difference for professionals in 1990 was especially sharp; 42 percent of all Jewish males were so employed compared to only 16 percent of white males. Jewish women were also more concentrated in white-collar positions and were disproportionally professional.

The occupational patterns of the various denominations largely reflect the national patterns, with some interesting differences (Table 15). Of those employed in 1990, either full- or part-time, six-in-ten Conservative men were in high white-collar positions (professionals or managers); and two-thirds of these were professionals. Only 14 percent were blue collar workers. Synagogue membership shows little differentiation in these occupational patterns.

By contrast, Orthodox Jews have a higher percentage of both professionals and blue collar workers and an especially low percentage of managers. A high percentage of Orthodox may have opted for professional positions because they may, thereby, have more flexible work schedules for observance of time-related rituals and shabbat/holidays. The Reform men, on the other hand, are more concentrated in the clerical/sales occupations and less so among professionals and blue-collar workers.

Among Conservative men, age is clearly related to occupation. The percentage of blue collar workers declines directly with age. These changes may be due either to upward occupational mobility over time or to changing opportunities for newer entrants into the labor force. The sharp drop among the elderly is, at least in part, due to the greater ease with which professionals can remain employed at older ages. Older men are also concentrated in the clerical/sales category. These are often part-time workers who are supplementing retirement income.

Perhaps most important from an institutional point of view is that between 40 and 50 percent of Conservative men under age 65 are professionals. This finding suggests that appeals to their loyalty must be made at a level appropriate to their high status. It also points to the potential for financial support that can be expected from a sizable segment of the Conservative population.

Women's occupational patterns generally parallel those of men, although a much larger percentage of women in every denomination are lower-level white-collar workers. Age differentials are striking among Conservative women. The youngest women are very heavily concentrated in lower-status occupations, perhaps because these women see their employment as temporary, preceding family formation and later career decisions. The pattern is radically different among the next older age groups. Women are heavily professional and managerial, apparently taking advantage of the opportunities for education and employment available to them in the last two decades. Like men, elderly women tend to hold clerical/sales jobs, most likely for similar reasons. That so many women in the middle-aged range, from which volunteers are usually drawn, are in high-level positions as professionals or managers underscores the constraints that synagogues and other institutions face in developing pools of volunteers.

The relation between age and occupational profile just discussed for Conservative Jewry as a whole characterizes individual communities as well. In addition, however, the local economic structure and employment opportunities appear to play an important role. Thus, over half of Conservative Jews in Columbus are concentrated among professionals, while in Dallas only one-third are professionals; but a disproportionate number are clerical/sales workers. San Francisco has a notably high proportion of managers (31 percent). These variations suggest that some localities are much more vulnerable to economic shifts than others and that local Conservative institutions may, therefore, also be more affected by economic changes in selected places.

Migration Patterns

Jews have participated fully in the mobility process that is such a dominant part of the American scene. Thus, migration is a key factor in helping to explain the distribution of the Jewish population among the regions of the United States. It is also a salient factor in accounting for the changing distribution of the population between metropolitan and nonmetropolitan areas and within metropolitan areas (Goldstein and Goldstein, 1996). In 1990, fewer than one-in-five adult Jews were living in the same town or city in which they were born; almost half of all adult Jews in 1990 were living in a state different from their state of birth. Another 10 percent were foreign-born.

Even if mobility is measured only over the five years preceding the 1990 survey, levels are high; about one-in-ten adult Jews had changed state of residence, and an equal proportion moved between communities within their home state. The high degree of movement suggests strongly that the impact of population movement must be taken into account in assessing the integration of Jews into the local Jewish community and in evaluating type and strength of Jewish identity. How closely do Conservative Jews follow these general patterns and how do they differ from the Orthodox and Reform Jews?

Since denominational affiliation is correlated with a range of socioeconomic variables as well with the extent of observance of a variety of religious practices, we expect denominational identity to be differentially associated with migration behavior. Observance of kashrut, sending children to religious school (especially a Jewish day school), having access to a mikveh, and having access to an appropriate synagogue/temple could all affect decisions about where to live and whether to migrate at all. Other things being equal, Orthodox and observant Conservative families and individuals may be the most stable, since their choice of locations is most restricted. Less observant Conservative Jews as well as Reform Jews and those who regard themselves as Just Jewish or Other may be more mobile because they have fewer observance-related constraints affecting their choice of residence. To test this expectation, two sets of data are used: (1) The lifetime migration measure is based on comparison of where the respondent was living at the times of the survey and where he or she was born; it does not indicate when the move occurred; and (2) The five-year migration measure is based on comparison of place of residence at the time of the survey in 1990 with residence five years earlier in 1985. Fuller attention will be given to the five-year measure since it relates to more recent movement.

Lifetime Migration. Conservative Jews clearly have higher levels of lifetime migration than the Orthodox Jews (Table 16). Fully 85 percent of Conservative adults, compared to only 68 percent of the

Figure 7 **Lifetime and Five-year Migration Status of Adult Conservative Jews**

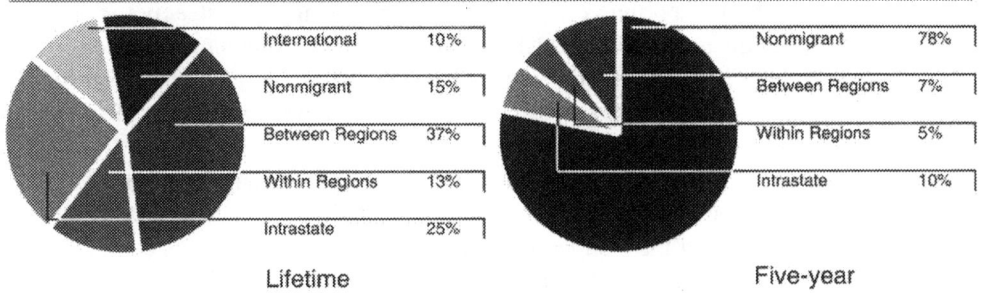

Lifetime	
International	10%
Nonmigrant	15%
Between Regions	37%
Within Regions	13%
Intrastate	25%

Five-year	
Nonmigrant	78%
Between Regions	7%
Within Regions	5%
Intrastate	10%

Orthodox adults, had changed community of residence between birth and 1990. Moreover, far more of the Conservative Jews moved across state boundaries compared to Orthodox Jews. Among those Conservative Jews who moved interstate, almost three times as many migrated from one region of the country to another as migrated within the same region, attesting to the major population redistribution that has characterized Conservative Jewry (Figure 7). Among the much lower proportion of Orthodox who had moved between states, the differential was much smaller. The Reform lifetime migration patterns were similar to those of the Conservatives, although fewer Reform Jews were born abroad. Adherence to a less traditional ideology is therefore clearly associated with higher levels of lifetime migration, especially within the United States.

Lifetime migration patterns vary widely among specific communities because of their unique development histories. Ninety-nine percent of the Conservative Jews of South Broward, for example, are either interstate migrants or were born abroad. In sharp contrast, lifetime stability is characteristic of Boston (where 62 percent were born in Massachusetts) and New York (with 78 percent born within state). The newer western Conservative communities are composed heavily of longer distance migrants; for example, 81 percent of San Francisco's Conservative Jews were not born in California.

Five-year Migration. The five-year migration data also show that Conservative and Reform Jews are more migratory than the Orthodox and move greater distances (Table 17). That more of those making an interstate move changed region of residence in the period 1985-1990 attests to the nationwide redistribution taking place even in this short interval (Figure 7).

Mobility is a striking feature of the experience of young Conservative adults. Over one-third had moved in the five years preceding the survey, and a majority of these migrants moved interstate; in fact, of the interstate migrants, more changed region of residence than moved within the same region. Most of the interstate migrants undoubtedly moved in connection with education, marriage, and job opportunities. The percentage moving drops steeply for the middle aged and the elderly. Yet, a majority of the movers in both these age cohorts migrated interstate, and most of these changed region of residence, probably in connection with retirement and the breakup of a home after the death of a spouse.

That five-year migration is so common among the younger segment of the Conservative adult population is significant for the strength of the Conservative movement. Mobility disrupts community ties (Goldstein and Goldstein, 1996) and is associated with lower levels of synagogue affiliation. The high mobility levels of persons who form the pool of future leaders of Conservative institutions, therefore, has serious implications. It is a major challenge to engage the interest and involvement of this group during a time in their lives when they are likely to have fewer ties to family, specific institutions, or community.

A number of factors may account for the relation between distance of move and affiliation. The overall ties of nonmembers to the Jewish community and to the general area may have been less strong than those of affiliated Conservative Jews. They also may have been more willing to move to areas that did not provide easy access to a synagogue. Even when a synagogue is available, such migrants may be slow in affiliating in their new place of residence. Finally, longer distance moves may be generally more disruptive of organizational ties.

If five-year mobility is especially associated with lower levels of integration into the local community, then variations in levels of such migration are especially important factors in community planning. The data available for individual communities show very similar patterns across most localities, with about one-fifth of Conservative Jews living in a different community in 1990 than in 1985. Some exceptions appear, most notably in Dallas and Seattle, where as many as one-third of the Conservative Jews were in-migrants. These comparatively high rates, especially for communities such as Dallas and Seattle, suggest that integration of migrants represents a major challenge.

Future Mobility. The challenge for Conservative Jewry is underscored by anticipated future mobility. When asked whether they expected to move in the three years following the survey, 44 percent of the Conservative Jews expected to do so, with just under half of these thinking a move was very likely (Table 18). Younger Jews were especially likely to anticipate moving in the future, but even among older age groups, anticipated future mobility is not unusual. Migration must, therefore, be a key factor in community planning; it calls for viewing the population in national rather than strictly local terms.

That roots in a community are intricately related to mobility behavior is further evidenced in the data showing anticipated mobility in relation to synagogue membership. Whereas 64 percent of the Conservative respondents belonging to affiliated households thought it unlikely that they would move in the next three years, just under half of the nonaffiliated thought likewise. Moreover, almost twice as many of the nonmembers as of the members reported it very likely that they would be geographically mobile in the near future.

Both lifetime and future mobility are thus associated with lower levels of synagogue membership, stressing the importance of programs designed to more fully integrate the mobile segment of Conservative Jewry into the institutional structure of the community. Failure to do so may result in having their mobility exacerbate weak ties to the Jewish community and further diminish their Jewish identity. The high rates of mobility among Conservative Jews, especially among those aged 18-44, should place this concern high on the agenda.

* * * * *

These data on the socioeconomic characteristics of the Conservative population in comparison to those in other denominations and to the nondenominational vividly illustrate the centrist position of Conservative Jewry. While Conservative Jews are likely to be religiously less stringent than Orthodox Jews and more so than Reform Jews, it is surprising that similar patterns hold for secular characteristics as well. The educational achievement of Conservative Jews and the percentage who hold mid-level occupations is higher than among Orthodox Jews but lower than among Reform Jews. Even the geographic mobility experiences of the three groups follows a similar pattern: Reform Jews are the most mobile and Orthodox Jews the least; Conservative Jews fall between the two but tend to be more like the Reform population than like the Orthodox. Because intermarriage is closely related to religious values and behavior, the centrist pattern found for both levels of and attitudes toward intermarriage among Conservative Jews is expected.

Within the Conservative population, age serves to further differentiate patterns. The younger population is clearly more educated than older Conservative Jews, although their occupational patterns are not as sharply distinct. Almost one-quarter of those under age 45 are not married. And the young married, in sharp contrast to older respondents, are most likely to be living in households with children under age 15. Among those who are married, those married in the 1980s (largely younger persons) were much more likely to be intermarried, reflecting changing attitudes toward choice of marriage partner. Younger persons were more supportive of intermarriage than the older population.

As younger Conservative Jews age and as the older population dies, these patterns are likely to change, or at least to be modified. Since they have clear implications for the leadership and general vitality of the Conservative movement, close monitoring of the situation is important so that programs can be responsive to changes in the socioeconomic composition of its adherents.

IV. Jewish Practices and Involvement

American Jewish religious denominations have distinctive and differing attitudes and practices. These differentials have important implications for individual Jewish identity and for the vitality and continuity of the American Jewish community. Over the years, a number of identifiable changes have been introduced by the Conservative movement (Wertheimer, 1989). They include the following: (1) Worship services that combine a high degree of fidelity to the traditional liturgy with innovations appropriate to the twentieth century are incorporated in the movement's own prayer books. (2) Part-time Hebrew schools and day schools provide more intensive schooling than is usually offered by the Reform movement. (3) Adherence to halakhah is maintained but modified through interpretations of the Conservative rabbinate's law committee so that Conservative interpretation of halakhah has departed significantly from that of Orthodox. Changed practices allow, for example, for mixed seating, equality of women in all aspects of synagogue life, and the ordination of women rabbis and cantors.

These practices distinguish the Conservative movement from Orthodox Judaism in which so many of the current Conservative Jews were raised. They are also substantially different from Reform Judaism. The Conservative movement is often considered as a "middle road" not as stringent as Orthodox, not as radically different as Reform. Yet, perhaps only a minority of persons classifying themselves as Conservative Jews actually adhere to the religious commitments and laws prescribed by the Conservative movement (*Emet ve-Emunah,* 1988).

NJPS-1990 collected a wide variety of information on how respondents and their households manifested their Jewish identity. This allows comparison of the Conservative population with the Orthodox and Reform populations in extent of Jewish education, practice of Jewish rituals, synagogue/temple membership and affiliation, participation in the formal organized life of the Jewish community, philanthropic giving, ties to Israel, and involvement in informal Jewish friendship and neighborhood networks. We begin by comparing the behavior of Conservative Jews with that of Jews in the other denominations, and by examining age and membership differences within Conservative Jewry.

Jewish Education
Jewish education is a key variable in determining Jewish identity. Previous research (Fishman and Goldstein, 1993) has shown that the

37

intensity of Jewish education, number of years and type in combination, is closely and directly related to a number of behavioral indicators of Jewish identity: Jewish organizational membership, philanthropic giving to Jewish causes, attitudes toward living in a Jewish milieu, extent of religious practices, and rates of intermarriage. To the extent that the denominations vary in the emphasis they place on Jewish education and in the types of educational programs they typically offer, we expect significant differences in the educational profiles of those affiliated with the Orthodox, Conservative, Reform, and Reconstructionist movements, and of those who do not identify with any movement. Moreover, since the types and intensity of educational programs sponsored by each group have changed substantially over the last half century, we also expect cohort differences among Conservative Jews.

Another key factor affecting the current profile of the Jewish educational attainment of Conservative Jews is the extent of switching that has occurred in denominational identity. Many "current" Conservatives, for example, may have been raised in Orthodox families and educated in Orthodox institutions. To fully assess such a relation requires in-depth attention to the relation between switching and past, as well as current, Jewish practices; data are not available for such an extensive analysis, but some of these issues will be touched on in our later discussion of denominational switching.

While formal Jewish schooling is obviously a key component of any Jew's education, informal opportunities — youth groups, camps, trips to Israel — also play an important role in shaping an individual's Jewish identity. NJPS-1990 collected information on informal activities only for children; we cannot, therefore, include this component of Jewish education in our analysis of adults. Research using the data for children (Goldstein and Fishman, 1993) suggests that informal education serves as a complement to more formal schooling, so that, for adults in 1990, the relation between intensity of formal Jewish education and other aspects of Jewish behavior is not distorted by omission of informal educational experiences.

For current purposes, the years/type of Jewish education are collapsed into four levels: none, low (less than 3 years of any religious schooling or 3-5 years of Sunday School only); medium (3-5 years of supplementary or day school or 6 years of Sunday school); high (6 years or more of either supplementary or day school). The results show that adult Conservative Jews differ significantly in their Jewish educational attainment from other Jews (Table 19). Almost one-quarter had no Jewish education at all, fairly similar to the 28 percent of Reform Jews without formal Jewish education. By contrast, only 15 percent of the Orthodox Jews reported no Jewish schooling. As expected, much higher proportions of those reporting themselves as Just Jewish or Other have no Jewish education.

Conservative Jews fall between Orthodox and Reform Jews in the proportion with a high level of Jewish education. Most Conservative adults attended supplementary schools. Many more of the Orthodox, by contrast, received their Jewish education in day schools. Conservative adults reporting a low level of Jewish schooling also place between the Orthodox and Reform. Among Reconstructionist Jews, the level of Jewish education is strikingly high; almost half are in the highest category and another quarter reported medium levels. Only 11 percent reported no Jewish schooling. Just the opposite pattern characterizes those with no denominational identification; the great majority of Just Jewish and of Other had no or only a low level of Jewish education.

For Conservative Jews, these data clearly point to an intermediary level of achievement in Jewish education. Apparently most of these respondents remained in religious school just long enough to celebrate their bar/bat mitzvah. We must especially recognize that one-third of Conservative adults have had no or only minimal Jewish education. The data also indicate wide variation in the educational experience of the Conservative group. Some of the differences are age-related — older women were especially likely to have had little formal education. Other differences are related to the varied Jewish background of those affiliated with the movement. The wide range in educational levels points to the need for a variety of programs, reaching all age groups, but especially adults, to fill some of the gaps resulting from the restricted Jewish education that Conservative Jews had as children.

Differences in level of Jewish education by synagogue membership status are indicative of how intensity of Jewish education impinges on other aspects of Jewish identity (Figure 8). Whereas only 13 percent of Conservative Jews whose families were synagogue members had no Jewish education, this was true of 31 percent of the nonmember respondents. At the other extreme of the educational hierarchy, 45 percent of the members had 6 or more years of either day school or supplementary school training compared to only one-quarter of the nonmembers.

The strong relation between Jewish education and synagogue membership becomes clearest through comparison of the rates of affiliation of Conservative Jews with different levels of Jewish education (data not in table). Only one in five of those with no Jewish education were members of synagogue-affiliated households. This doubles for those in the low education category. It increases sharply for those characterized by a high level of Jewish education, among

39

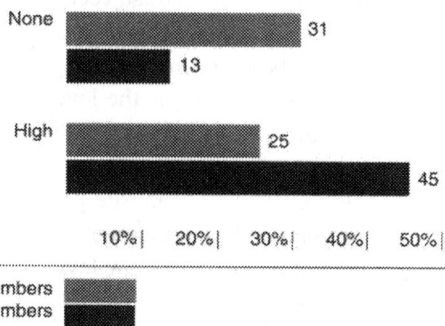

Figure 8 **Index of Jewish Education, Conservative Members and Nonmembers**

whom three times as many (60 percent) were affiliated as were those with no Jewish education. The data on earlier affiliation of the current nonmembers show that few of those Conservative Jews with no Jewish education ever belonged to a synagogue (only one in five), compared to 40-50 percent of those nonmembers with varying levels of Jewish education. For the latter, disaffiliation varied inversely with level of education.

Since education preceded recent membership, one can assume that either education in itself or other background/attitudinal factors associated with educational achievement account for these sharp differences. Nonetheless, a substantial proportion of "highly" educated Jews are among the nonmembers. Insights into why Conservative Jews with this type of earlier exposure to Judaism have opted not to belong to a synagogue should be useful for attracting many of them to affiliate.

Opportunities for Jewish education and incentives for enrollment have changed substantially over the decades. Supplementary schools have enriched their programs, Schechter Day Schools have proliferated, and access to other day school programs has increased. Different age cohorts of the Conservative population should, therefore, vary in their levels of Jewish educational attainment. Data not presented here, for example, show that the gender gap in Jewish education has virtually closed. Whereas 39 percent of elderly men had high levels of Jewish education, compared to only 20 percent of elderly women, among the youngest age group the proportions were identical at about 63 percent.

Age differences are apparent, especially between the elderly and those under age 65 (Figure 9). Over one-third of older persons

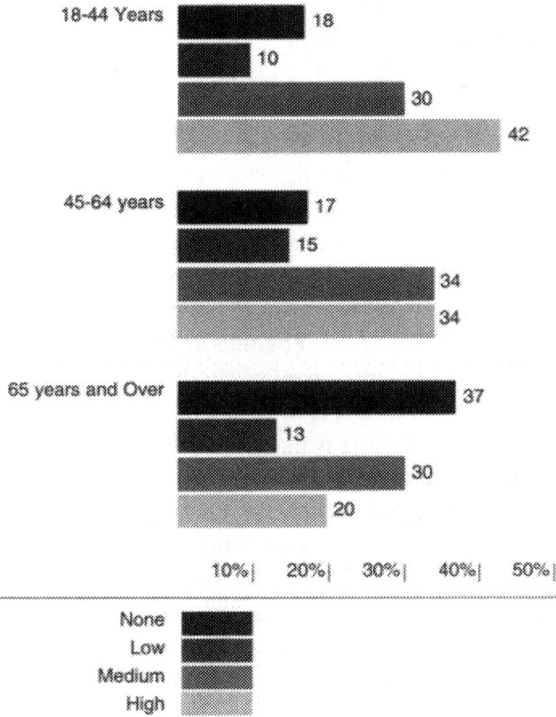

Figure 9 Index of Jewish Education for Adult Conservative Jews, by Age

18-44 Years
18
10
30
42

45-64 years
17
15
34
34

65 years and Over
37
13
30
20

10%| 20%| 30%| 40%| 50%|

None
Low
Medium
High

reported having had no formal Jewish education, and only one-fifth were in the high category. By contrast, only half as many of those under age 65 (17 percent) reported no schooling at all. While this represents a considerable improvement over the experience of the elderly, that the proportion is similar for those aged 45-64 and those aged 18-44 suggests considerable stability, with almost one-in-five Conservative Jews having no Jewish education. The proportion in the low education category varied less sharply by age, ranging only between 10 and 14 percent. Thus, over one-quarter of the youngest group had no or only a low level of Jewish education.

More encouraging is that the proportion with a high level of education increased from only one in five among the elderly to just over one-third of those aged 45-64 and 42 percent of those aged 18-44. Clearly, among the youngest cohort, those who received some education were more likely to remain in religious school beyond their bar/bat mitzvah years. Since the NJPS-1990 respondents received their Jewish education before Schechter Day Schools experienced their greatest expansion, our data do not reflect changes in the Conservativeauspices education of the 1980s and 1990s. We would expect in the future a somewhat higher percentage of Conservative adults reporting a more intensive Jewish education. As of 1990, however, a very large segment of Conservative Jewry had had only a moderate Jewish schooling; programs to serve this population will be vital to retain the strength of the movement.

Some indication of the future patterns of adult Jewish education can be gleaned from information in NJPS-1990 on the children currently living in Conservative households (data not in tables). These suggest that only a small minority (under 10 percent) of children were enrolled in day schools at the time of the survey; the one exception to this pattern is the 6-7 age group, among whom almost one-fourth are in full-time programs. The relatively high percentage of very young children in day schools may result from the kinds of programs that are available — preschool programs or those limited to the early grades. They form a potential pool of children who may continue with day school education if it is available in their community.

Most startling is that over one-third of children in the immediate pre-bar/bat mitzvah years (ages 8-12) were not currently enrolled in any program of Jewish education. Of the two-thirds enrolled, nine in ten were in part-time programs. Enrollment drops even further among teens, down to 49 percent of those aged 13-15 and to 24 percent of the 16-18 year olds. In many communities, high-school-level programs of Jewish study are not available; and where they are, the large majority of teens do not enroll. The lack of continuity of Jewish education beyond age 13 is a major challenge for the Conservative movement. Education limited to the elementary level is clearly inadequate for meaningful participation of adults in the life of the Conservative synagogue.

Synagogue Attendance

In addition to synagogue membership, attendance at synagogue services serves as an index of Jewish practices.[6] Not surprisingly, Orthodox Jews report the greatest frequency of synagogue attendance; just over half claimed they attend often (Table 20). Only about half as many Conservative Jews did so, and still fewer of the Reform Jews. Understandably, attendance rates were lowest for the Just Jewish and the Other. The limited role that synagogue attendance plays in the lives of Conservative Jews is evidenced in the fact that almost half reported that they attended services only seldom or not at all. This contrasted with one-third of Orthodox Jews and as many as six-in-ten Reform Jews.

---

6. Attendance was categorized as Never; Seldom (High Holy Days or only on special occasions); Occasionally (a few times a year); Often (once a month or more).

Attendance at synagogue services by Conservative Jews is highly correlated with membership in a synagogue. Half of all the members reported attending often, but only 11 percent of the nonmembers did so. One-in-five members indicated they seldom or never attended services, whereas just over two-thirds of the nonmembers reported such infrequent attendance. Whether belonging to a synagogue is conducive to greater attendance or whether those who want such involvement opt to join warrants further attention.

Age is related to frequency of attendance at synagogue services. Half or more of those in each age group reported attending occasionally or often, but more frequent attendance increases with age. One-quarter of Conservative adults under age 45 reported attending at least once a month, compared to one-third of those among the middle-aged group and the elderly. The young and the elderly share the distinction of having the largest proportion of nonattendees.

Ritual Practices

Community studies have shown that denominational affiliation and the extent of conformity to traditional ritual practices are correlated (Goldscheider and Goldstein, 1988; Israel, 1987). The denominations tend to form a continuum from Orthodox to Conservative to Reconstructionist to Reform to Just Jewish, paralleling their theological positions and ideologies. NJPS-1990 collected information on observances of a variety of ritual practices, which allows assessment of denominational differences as well as the extent of variation in observance among Conservative Jews. Information on ritual practices largely refers to the household as a whole, although a few questions were asked specifically of respondents.

Observance of Shabbat is at the very heart of Judaism, and lighting candles is one important aspect of that observance. Yet of Jewish respondents in NJPS-1990, only 17 percent reported that candles were either always or usually lit in their homes, while 62 percent reported never lighting candles (Table 21). Even among Conservative Jews, far more reported never lighting candles (49 percent) than reported doing so always or usually (23 percent). Among Orthodox Jews, 51 percent indicated that candles were always/usually lit for Shabbat, and only 30 percent reported this was never done. The opposite pattern characterizes Reform Jews, with only 10 percent reporting lighting candles always/usually and 67 percent never. Reconstructionist Jews closely paralleled the Conservative Jews, and the Just Jewish were most similar to Reform Jews. These data suggest that for almost half of Conservative Jews, as for a substantial minority of Orthodox Jews, lighting Shabbat candles is no longer part of the tradition, despite its importance in the ideology of these two movements and the importance attached to it as a way of reinforcing Jewish values and practices in the home.

Observance of Kashrut is defined as always purchasing kosher meat and using separate dishes for meat and dairy foods. Kashrut is clearly ignored more than it is observed. Among all Jews, only 10 percent had kosher households; the percentage varied widely by denomination. Among Conservative Jews, for whom kashrut is a halakhic requirement, only 15 percent reported following the dietary laws. Not surprisingly, a majority of Orthodox respondents reported a kosher home. Reform Judaism does not require adherence to the practice of kashrut, and only 2 percent of Reform respondents reported living in households that kept kosher. Both the Reconstructionist Jews and the Just Jewish quite closely resembled the Reform Jews.

In contrast to observance of kashrut and lighting Shabbat candles, observance of other ritual practices is much higher. Respondents were asked whether they themselves fasted on Yom Kippur. A majority in each of the four denominations (ranging from half of Reform Jews to 85 percent of Orthodox Jews) reported doing so always or usually. Seven-in-ten adult Conservative Jews reported always or usually fasting on Yom Kippur. About one in five of the Just Jewish fasted on Yom Kippur, consistent with their generally secular orientation.

Observing Passover through attendance at a seder and lighting Hanukkah candles have been the most common practices reported in community surveys. The seder is popular both because its celebration of liberation is in consonance with American principles of freedom and because it is seen primarily as a vehicle reinforcing the importance of family. For some, the observance of Passover at about the time when the larger community is celebrating Easter also makes the holiday, and especially the seder, attractive. Fully 64 percent of the respondents reported that their households always/usually attended a seder. Yet, almost one in five indicated they never did so, suggesting that a substantial number of Jews forego this family/religious event.

Hanukkah, like seder attendance, has come to be one of the most popular observances among Jewish Americans. Although it is a minor holiday, its temporal coincidence with Christmas has transformed it into an occasion for family celebration that in many ways mimics Christian observances. Almost four times as many respondents reported that Hanukkah candles were always/usually lit in their homes as reported lighting Shabbat candles; only one-quarter reported never lighting Hanukkah candles.

Because they are so widely popular, attendance at a seder and lighting Hanukkah candles show less variation among denominations than do lighting Shabbat candles, keeping kosher, and fasting on Yom

Kippur. The percentage reporting attendance at a seder always/usually varied only between 70 percent and 74 percent for three major denominations, with Conservative Jewry at the highest level and Reform Jewry at the lowest. Even more Reconstructionist Jews (81 percent) reported seder attendance. Among the Just Jewish, seder attendance was the most often reported ritual (42 percent), and fewer Just Jewish respondents indicated that they never observed this ritual than any other ritual reported here. Virtually the same patterns of high levels of observance and minimum differentials among denominations characterize Hanukkah candle lighting.

Sharp differences in ritual practice characterized synagogue members and nonmembers among Conservative Jews (Figure 10). For every practice discussed, nonmembers reported sharply lower levels of observance than members. For example, as low as the frequency of lighting Shabbat candles and observing Kashrut were among Conservatives Jews, these practices were always/usually practiced by even lower proportions of nonmembers, only 11 percent and 6 percent, respectively, compared to 37 percent and 25 percent of members. A small majority of nonmembers fasted on Yom Kippur, attended a seder, and lit Hanukkah candles. By contrast, about 90 percent of the members adhered to each of these practices. Religious commitment as evidenced by synagogue membership is thus clearly correlated with the extent of ritual observance. Persons who follow ritual practices are apparently most likely to affiliate with a synagogue, but it is also possible that membership may lead to higher levels of observance through the stimulation provided by the educational programs, peer pressure, and involvement in synagogue-related

Figure 10 Percent Following Selected Ritual Practices, Conservative Members and Nonmembers

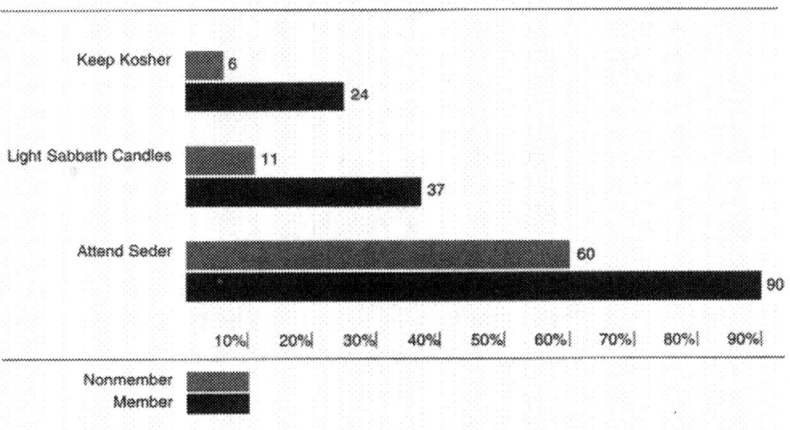

activities.

A Ritual Practices Index, incorporating levels of observance of the five practices, was constructed to provide a summary measure on which the denominations could be compared and to facilitate evaluation of segments of the Conservative population. Individual practices were weighted to reflect the intensity with which they are observed. (See Appendix B for how the index was constructed.) In turn, the scores were used to establish four categories of level of practice: none, low, medium, and high.

Consistent with our findings for specific rituals, Conservative Jews tend to be intermediary in overall level of observance (Table 22). One-fourth of Conservative Jews scored high on the index, compared to two-thirds of Orthodox Jews and just 8 percent of Reform Jews. Reconstructionist Jews closely resembled the Conservatives. About the same proportion (4 to 6 percent) in the three major denominations scored none, indicating total nonobservance of the rituals included. More Conservative Jews scored in the medium category than in any other, very close to the pattern of Reconstructionist Jews. Reform Jews were about equally divided between medium and low. The Just Jewish were heavily concentrated in the low category.

Like the differentials by membership status for specific practices, the index was consistently higher for synagogue members than for nonmembers. The proportion of Conservative Jews reported as affiliated with synagogues increases regularly and steeply with increasing scores on the ritual index. This pattern extends to former membership (data not in table). Whereas only 6 percent of Conservative nonmembers who scored zero on the ritual index formerly belonged, as many as 57 percent of the nonmembers scoring high on the Index were formerly affiliated. Observance and membership, current or earlier, are closely correlated. The major question confronting researchers and planners is what leads individuals who identify themselves as Conservative to ignore the norms, halakhic and otherwise, of their movement, including both ritual observance and synagogue membership.

Life-cycle stages can obviously influence the extent to which certain rituals and practices are observed. Aged persons in poor health may not fast on Yom Kippur or even be able to attend a seder. Having children in the household is a powerful stimulant for the observance of Hanukkah. If children in the family are enrolled in day schools, ritual observance in general may rise. The data by age for Conservative Jews point to differences in extent of observance, especially between the middle-aged and the younger segments of the population (Figure 11).

About three in ten of the elderly and those aged 45-64 had high ritual practice scores, compared to only 21 percent of the youngest

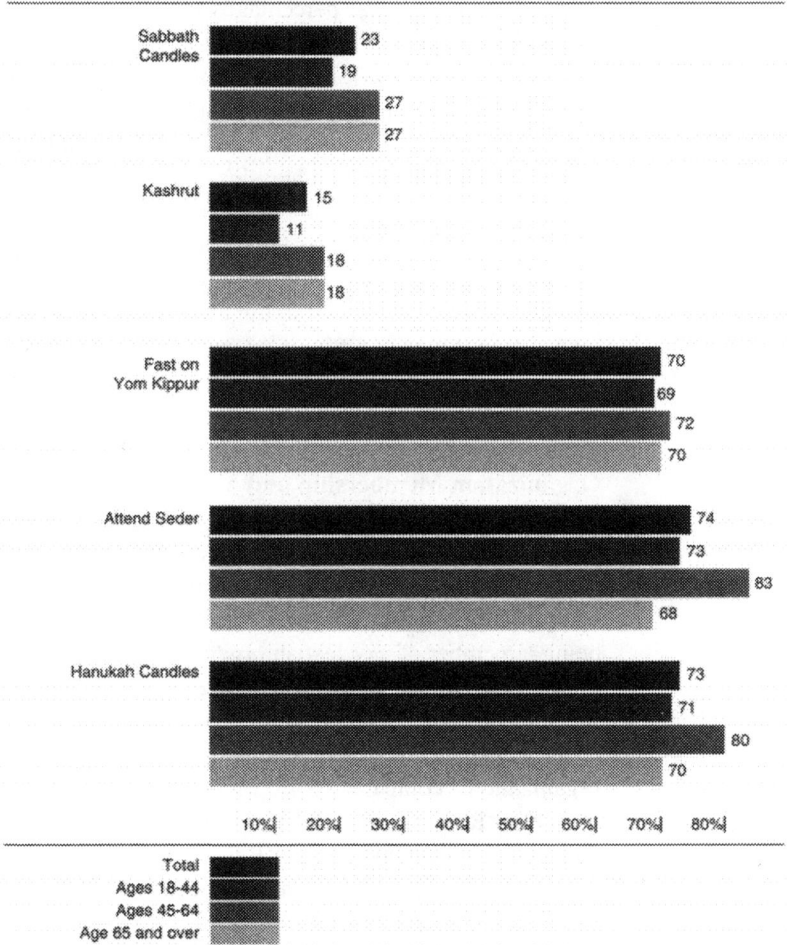

Figure 11 **Percent of Conservative Adults Whose Households Always/Usually Perform Selected Rituals, by Age**

Ritual	Total	Ages 18-44	Ages 45-64	Age 65 and over
Sabbath Candles	23	19	27	27
Kashrut	15	11	18	18
Fast on Yom Kippur	70	69	72	70
Attend Seder	74	73	83	68
Hanukah Candles	73	71	80	70

group. The low proportion of young with high scores and their concomitantly greater concentration in the low/none categories may in part be a life-cycle effect that might change over time as this cohort ages and comes into different family situations. It may also, however, portend a weakening of ritual observance, a trend that is generally mirrored in the age patterns of specific ritual practices. Only longitudinal analysis will provide full answers to the reasons and implications of the observed cross-sectional patterns. In the meantime, the organized Conservative community should make concerted efforts to educate the younger segment of the population to the value of greater observance.

Despite our findings about the relation of age to observance of ritual practices, the community data suggest that for Conservative Jews regional location has an extremely strong influence. Communities in the West, and even Columbus, score consistently lower on the Ritual Practices Index. Lower percentages score high (12-19 percent) and larger percentages are in the medium range (64-74 percent) than is true of communities in the East. Scores of low or none show minimal variation across communities, although South Broward and Dallas have fewer of their Conservative population scoring low (12-13 percent) than do other communities. These regional patterns suggest that Conservative Jews who moved away from the more traditional East Coast cities were either less observant before their move or found the new location conducive to a relaxation of ritual practices. The general ambiance produced in the older areas of settlement, with their higher proportions of Orthodox Jews and easier access to Jewish facilities like kosher markets, may also make it easier to be more observant.

Organization Membership and Volunteer Activities

Jewish identity can also express itself through participation in the organized life of the broader Jewish community, in terms of membership in Jewish organizations other than synagogues and volunteer activity (Table 23). Only 30 percent of all Jews reported being a member of any Jewish organization other than a synagogue/temple. Again, the adherents of the three denominations vary considerably along the anticipated continuum.

Four-in-ten Conservative adults belonged to one or more Jewish organizations, compared to 43 percent of Orthodox Jews and only 28 percent of Reform Jews. Reconstructionist Jews have a level of participation just above that of Reform Jews, but the Just Jewish and Others, consistent with our earlier findings, had very low participation rates. Interestingly, more Conservative Jews (47 percent) are active in non-Jewish (secular) organizations than in Jewish organizations.[7] This is also true of the Reform, Reconstructionist, and nondenominational Jews. Only among the Orthodox Jews do fewer participate in secular organizations (30 percent) than in Jewish ones. The inverse relation between rates of participation in Jewish groups and in non-Jewish groups among the varied denominations suggests that the lower the level of identity with traditional Judaism, the higher the levels of integration into the larger community.

Participation in Jewish organizations is correlated with membership in a synagogue. Over twice as high a proportion of

7. Data on non-Jewish organizational membership, voluntarism, and philanthropy are not shown in Table 23.

Conservative respondents whose households were synagogue members belonged to one or more other Jewish organizations than did nonsynagogue members. Synagogue members were also more active in non-Jewish organizations than were nonmembers, but the differential was not as great as for Jewish organizations. The level of activity of nonmembers in non-Jewish organizations was considerably greater than in Jewish organizations. This suggests that nonmembers of synagogues are more involved in the organizational life of the larger community than in that of the Jewish community.

That synagogue members are more heavily involved than nonmembers in both Jewish and non-Jewish organizations suggests that Jews who integrate into a community's institutional structure do so at many levels, including synagogues, Jewish organizations, and secular organizations. Nonmembers tend to be generally less involved in the community, especially in the Jewish sector.

Denominational differences, similar to those characterizing organizational activity, also characterize Jewish volunteer activity; but the differences are greater and the overall levels of participation are lower. Only about one-quarter of the Conservative Jews reported volunteering for Jewish causes. By contrast, one-third of the Orthodox Jews engaged in such voluntarism, while only 16 percent of the Reform Jews did so. Reconstructionist Jews more closely resembled the Orthodox on this index, but again the Just Jewish and Others engaged minimally in Jewish volunteer work.

As with organizational membership, more Conservative Jews engage in secular volunteer activity than in Jewish voluntarism. The same is true of adults in all other denominational and nondenominational categories, except for the Orthodox adults. The generally inverse relation between the degree of denominational traditionalism on the one hand and the level of involvement in secular voluntarism on the other — and the direct relation of denominational traditionalism to level of activity in Jewish voluntarism — again points to the greater integration of less traditional Jews in the larger community and their lesser degree of commitment to Jewish causes.

For Conservative Jews, synagogue membership was associated with much higher rates of volunteer activity; four-in-ten Conservative Jews whose household belonged to a synagogue reported volunteer activity compared to only 11 percent of nonmembers. Moreover, whereas 42 percent of former members of synagogues were active in Jewish volunteer work, only one-third of those former members were not active as volunteers. These differences may stem from volunteer work being an outgrowth of synagogue membership, but other underlying factors related to Jewish identity may also account for both higher membership rates and greater Jewish volunteer activity.

Synagogue membership was also associated with higher levels of volunteer activity in secular causes. Virtually identical proportions of Conservative synagogue members were active in secular volunteer activities as in Jewish ones, suggesting that membership per se is correlated with a commitment to volunteer activity, regardless of its religio-secular character. By contrast, nonmembers were far less likely to volunteer in Jewish activities than in secular activities. Clearly, not being a synagogue member is associated with more involvement in non-Jewish volunteer work, just as it was correlated with a higher level of participation in non-Jewish organizations.

Life-cycle stage, as indexed by age, is associated with levels of involvement in the formal Jewish organizational structure. Younger Conservative Jews are less active than older persons. The differences are sharper for organization membership than for voluntarism. The lower levels among the elderly are not surprising, since many may be physically constrained so that active volunteer work becomes impossible for them. The overall lower levels of the youngest group may be a cause for concern. Unless ways can be found to involve these Jews more actively as they move into later stages of the life cycle, the volunteer sector of the Jewish community will suffer a serious dearth of participants.

Involvement in the organized Jewish community shows great variation in organization membership levels among localities but little differentiation when voluntarism is considered. Whereas six out of ten Conservative Jews in Boston and Rhode Island reported membership in Jewish organizations, just under half in San Francisco and Seattle reported such membership; New York and South Broward had even lower levels of organizational membership (about one-third). While an East-West split seems to be operating here as it does for other characteristics, the unique populations of New York and South Broward also play an important role. Older age, immigrant status, and Jewish population density may all be explanatory factors.

In contrast to the variation in synagogue membership, levels of Jewish voluntarism are fairly similar across communities, ranging only between 34 percent and 44 percent. No distinctive geographic pattern appears. The very low level for South Broward may be easily explained in terms of the high proportion of elderly in the population, for whom volunteer activities may be physically prohibitive.

Philanthropy

Still another expression of Jewish identity and commitment to the community is represented by charitable donations to Jewish causes (Rimor and Tobin, 1991; Kosmin and Ritterband, 1991). Half of all Jewish respondents in NJPS-1990 reported giving to Jewish causes in the year preceding the 1990 survey (Table 23). The denominational differences that exist for philanthropy are similar to those for Jewish organizational membership and volunteer activity. The Conservative level of giving (63 percent) was intermediate between Orthodox (72 percent) and the Reform (50 percent). Again, Reconstructionist Jews resembled the Conservative Jews, and Just Jewish and Other had much lower levels of giving to Jewish causes. Thus, even while concern for fellow Jews is a value that cuts across denominational lines, it tends to be weaker for the less traditional denominations.

A pattern of denominational differences also characterizes contributions to non-Jewish causes. The percentage of Conservative Jews giving to a secular cause (65 percent) is quite similar to the 63 percent giving to Jewish causes. However, fewer Orthodox Jews give to secular causes (55 percent) than to Jewish ones, and the reverse is true of the Reform Jews. Far more of the Reconstructionist Jews (80 percent), the Just Jewish (64 percent), and the Other (65 percent) give to non-Jewish causes than to Jewish ones.

For Conservative Jews, level of giving is relatively high in all communities — from two-thirds to almost all — related in large part to the effectiveness of local fund-raising efforts. Nonetheless, some differences are apparent, consistent with previously noted differences in community involvement. The highest levels of giving are reported for the communities in the East and South Broward (New York is an exception), while lower levels prevail in the Midwest and the West.

Again, sharp differentials exist between Conservative Jews whose households hold synagogue membership and those whose households do not. Eight-in-ten members report making contributions to Jewish causes, but only half of nonmembers do so. Moreover, among the nonmembers, over half who were contributors had been synagogue members at some time in the past; but only 19 percent who did not give had ever belonged to a synagogue (data not shown in tables). Part of this very large differential may be accounted for by the inclusion of membership dues as contributions, even though NJPS-1990 specifically asked that dues and memberships be excluded from the responses. Nonetheless, members are clearly more likely to make a financial commitment to Jewish organizations. Interestingly, the same general pattern of differentials in level of synagogue membership characterizes contributions to secular causes.

Age is also a strong differentiating factor in Jewish giving. Only half of the youngest age group of Conservative Jews report contributions, compared to about three-quarters of the others. A very clear pattern thus emerges from these data on involvement in the organized Jewish community of much lower levels of commitment on the part of younger Conservative Jews compared to the middle-aged and older groups. Whether younger Jews will become more involved later in their lives remains speculative. From the community's perspective, they should clearly be the target of concerted efforts for leadership development and greater commitment.

Israel Visits

The last indicator of involvement in the formal Jewish community examined here is ties to Israel as evidenced by ever having visited the Jewish state (Table 23). Just over one-quarter of all adult Jews reported making such visits. The now-familiar denominational pattern holds for visits to Israel. While 37 percent of Conservative adults had made such a visit, this was true of 53 percent of Orthodox adults and only 23 percent of Reform adults. The Reconstructionist Jews closely resembled the Conservative Jews, and the Just Jewish were similar to the Reform. Fewer than 10 percent of the Others had ever visited Israel.

Among Conservative Jews, synagogue membership was associated with much higher rates of visits to Israel; almost half of the members, but only about one-quarter of the nonaffiliated, had visited. The affiliated may have more opportunities for making such trips; synagogues often encourage congregants to visit Israel and, in fact, often organize such trips.

Differences in visits to Israel may partially reflect a life-cycle effect or the greater time that the elderly have had for such a trip and the greater financial resources that may be available to them. Whatever the reason, a higher percentage of the elderly than of the youngest group reports having visited Israel. The youngest group reports the lowest levels. This is somewhat surprising since in recent decades many programs have been sponsored by synagogues/temples, youth groups, local federations, and others to encourage young Jews to go to Israel. That only about one-third of Conservative Jews aged 18-44 have ever been to Israel means that only a comparatively small segment of potential visitors in this age group have yet had an Israel experience. Whether it reflects less "feeling" for Israel because the youngest cohort was born after the Holocaust and after the struggle for Israel Independence (many were even born after the Six-Day War) needs to be explored with data beyond NJPS-1990. This possibility must be taken into account, however, not only in exploring the reasons for lower levels of travel to Israel, but also in explaining lower levels of Jewish identity as evidenced by other indicators.

A very clear pattern thus emerges from these data on involvement in the organized Jewish community of much lower levels of commitment on the part of younger self-identified Conservative Jews compared to the middle-aged and older groups. Whether younger Jews will become more involved later in their lives cannot be determined from the data at hand. They should clearly be the target of concerted efforts for greater commitment and leadership development. Affiliation and participation in synagogues are clearly channels for stimulating more visits.

Jewish Milieu

Ties to the community can take different forms. Participation in the formal, organized life of the community and observance of a variety of Jewish practices are not the only manifestations of Jewish identity. Having Jewish friends and living in Jewish neighborhoods also indicate the strength of individual identification with the larger community and provide a mechanism for maintaining that identity. Indeed, some scholars have maintained that as the more traditional indices of identity and cohesion diminish in importance, the informal ones represented by choice of friends, neighborhood, and even colleagues at work assume complementary or substitute roles as mechanisms for insuring continuity in individual identity and maintaining ties to the larger Jewish community (Goldscheider, 1986: 165-169).

For a good part of their history in the United States, Jews have adjusted to life in America by residential clustering. Doing so made it easier for them to maintain their Jewish identity through close, daily interaction with other Jews and easy access to facilities essential for a Jewish life style, observance of religious rituals, and the religious/cultural education of their children. Residential clustering was also a reaction to anti-Semitism and restrictive property covenants, which made it difficult or even impossible for Jews to live in certain neighborhoods.

After World War II, Jews participated in the widespread national migration and residential mobility processes in the United States. Jewish residential clustering declined as Jews joined the movement to the suburbs and also moved to a wider set of metropolitan and even nonmetropolitan areas, many of which lacked established areas of high Jewish density. The Jewish population within metropolitan areas has, as a result, become more dispersed. Concurrently, in many metropolitan areas, Jewish institutions have relocated at widely separated points, and often at considerable distances from much of the population they are intended to serve. This dispersal of both population and institutions contributes to weakening the Jewish ties that deeper residential roots fostered in the past.

Sensitive to these concerns about the role of informal ties in strengthening Jewish identity, NJPS-1990 collected information on a variety of indicators of the Jewish milieu, including Jewish friendship patterns and Jewish character of neighborhood. Among all adults in the sample, over one-third reported that among their closest friends all or most were Jewish. Only 8 percent reported having no Jews among their closest friends. Perhaps indicative of trends toward greater integration into the larger community, the proportion reporting most or all of their friends Jewish declined from six in ten of the elderly to only 27 percent of those aged 18-44. By contrast, the percentage with no Jewish friends rose from 4 percent of the elderly to 10 percent of the younger group.

Evidencing the type of historical changes noted earlier in Jewish residential patterns, only 9 percent of Jewish respondents reported living in what they regarded as very Jewish neighborhoods, just over one-quarter were in somewhat Jewish neighborhoods, and as many as 62 percent were in neighborhoods with few or no Jews. Moreover, the differences between age groups were sharp, with just under half of elderly Jews living in neighborhoods of very low Jewish density compared to almost seven-in-ten Jews aged 18-44.

Respondents were also asked how much importance they attached to the Jewish character of the neighborhood in which they lived. Almost half thought it very important, but 30 percent did not believe it was at all important. Interestingly, while the proportion considering it very important declined from 54 percent of the elderly to 44 percent of those aged 18-44, minimum differences characterized the age groups with respect to the proportion saying it was not important.

In this analysis of Conservative Jews, we assess the joint importance of Jewish friends and Jewish neighborhood (both density and importance) through use of a Jewish Milieu Index based on all three indicators.[8]

Reflecting a combination of many factors, including observance of Shabbat and kashrut, Jewish education of children, socioeconomic status, age, and generation status, the members of the denominations vary considerably in how they scored on the index (Table 24). One-third of the Conservative Jews placed in the high category. While this was far below the 51 percent of Orthodox Jews, it was over twice as high as for Reform Jews, and also far greater than for the Reconstructionist Jews. The Just Jewish and Other had only a small proportion in this high category, pointing to their far greater integration into the non-Jewish community. Conversely, the 28 percent of Conservative Jews who scored low on the index fell between the percentages for the Orthodox and Reform Jews; far higher

---

8. Each indicator of the index was given a score of 0 to 2, and the index was constructed to equal the sum of the scores; it has a range of 0 to 6, with a higher score indicating greater Jewish intensity. Based on the scores, three categories of intensity were established — low (0-2), medium (3-4), high (5-6).

percentages of the Just Jewish and Other scored low on the Jewish Milieu Index. Thus, Conservative Jews were almost equally divided among the three categories, whereas more of the Orthodox were in the high group and more of the Reform in the low category. For most self-identified Conservative Jews, Jewish milieu as represented by friends and neighborhood is apparently not particularly important and, therefore, for many is not likely to serve as a major mechanism for enhancing or reinforcing Jewish identity.

Such a conclusion also flows from the data by age. Reflecting younger Jews' generally lower level of Jewish residential concentration and lower number of Jewish friends, sharp differences in the Jewish Milieu Index characterized the three age cohorts of Conservative Jews. Whereas half of the elderly scored high, this declines to only 37 percent of the middle-aged and still fewer (24 percent) of those aged 18-44. At the other extreme, the percentage operating in a low Jewish milieu rises from one-in-five elderly Conservative Jews to just over one-third of the youngest group.

A shift from higher to lower exposure to other Jews through friendships and/or neighborhood appears to have occurred. Whether this will persist as younger Jews move on to later stages of the life cycle remains to be seen. There seems no strong reason to believe, however, that, for those who have established peripherally Jewish friendships and residential patterns, these patterns will later be reversed in favor of more intense Jewish environments, especially given the general patterns of movement and occupational mobility.

Scores achieved on the Jewish Milieu Index are highly correlated with synagogue membership. Among members, 43 percent scored high, while only 21 percent scored low. By contrast, only 28 percent of the nonmembers were in the high category of the Jewish Milieu Index, but 34 percent scored low. Quite clearly for Conservative Jews, living within a Jewish environment is closely associated with synagogue membership. It is also associated with earlier membership of nonmember Conservative Jews. Only 18 percent of the nonmembers scoring low on the Jewish Milieu Index were former members, whereas 56 percent of those scoring high had held earlier affiliation. Apparently, membership is in part associated with factors other than a Jewish milieu. Financial considerations and attitudes toward formal institutions may also play a role.

* * * * *

The centrist position of Conservative Jews on a variety of socioeconomic characteristics is even more apparent when religious behavioral variables are considered. The levels of Jewish education, synagogue attendance, ritual practices, involvement in the organized

Jewish community, and living in a Jewish milieu are for Conservative Jews intermediate between the levels for Orthodox and Reform Jews. The great behavioral deviation from practices that are central to Conservative Judaism, like lighting Shabbat candles or maintaining kashrut, points to the diversity of belief and the divergence from the stated Conservative norms in much of the religious behavior of persons who identify with the denomination. Our findings, thus, highlight the inclusion within the movement of adherents with widely differing levels of religious behavior.

The range of denominational differences is narrower for variables related to involvement in the formal structure of the Jewish community. Nonetheless, the level of membership in Jewish organizations, voluntarism for Jewish activities, and giving to Jewish causes among Conservative Jews is consistently intermediary between that of Orthodox and Reform Jews.

Within the Conservative population, age is a strong factor in accounting for levels of behavior. The youngest group of Conservative respondents is distinctive in having not only very high levels of secular education but relatively high levels of Jewish education as well. The notably low levels among the elderly are due in large part to the lack of women's Jewish education in the past. The higher levels of Jewish education among younger Conservative Jews do not, however, translate directly into higher levels of synagogue attendance, ritual observance, or involvement in the Jewish community. The mixed patterns suggest that younger people are quite selective about what they choose to observe and how they choose to identify with the Jewish community. Stage of life cycle undoubtedly also has a strong influence on identificational behavior, in which case patterns may change as younger persons develop careers and live in different family situations. Changes in the future may also reflect the impact of Schechter Day Schools, Jewish-auspices summer camps, and Israel trips on increasing numbers of young people.

Finally, synagogue membership is clearly and unsurprisingly associated with much higher levels of ritual practices and involvement in the formal structure of the Jewish community. And members, much more than nonmembers, consider a Jewish milieu to be important to them. Persons who identify as Conservative Jews and are affiliated with a synagogue, therefore, form an important subset of the entire Conservative population. It is important to remember, however, that an equally large number of persons identify themselves as Conservative Jews even though they are not affiliated with a synagogue. They constitute a potential reservoir of synagogue members.

V. Across the Regional Spectrum

The regional distribution of Conservative Jews in comparison to those in other denominations has been described earlier. For the three major denominations, the Northeast was the major region of residence, and the Midwest contained the smallest proportion. Conservative and Reform Jews were about equally represented in the South and the West, while Orthodox Jews were by far the most heavily concentrated in the Northeast.

Regional distribution is significant for several reasons: (1) If it is the result of the wide dispersion of the Jewish population, regional distribution affects the ease with which national services can be provided and a sense of national community can be maintained. (2) If the sociodemographic characteristics of the populations differ by region of residence, then the distribution can affect the nature of Jewish identity and call for quite different types of services from national and regional agencies. (3) Similarly, if the populations living in the varied regions differ substantially in their basic Judaic commitments and practices, their needs for and use of services and institutions will differ. (4) Finally, because the regions themselves vary in socioenvironmental conditions, each provides a quite different context within which the Jewish community functions. In the analysis that follows, we compare Conservative Jews living in the four regions in terms of their basic sociodemographic characteristics and on a variety of behavioral indicators of Jewish identity.

Migration

Many of the changes in the distribution of Conservative Jews are attributable to migration. Conservative Jews, like other Jews and the larger American population, have moved interregionally in response to economic opportunities, life-cycle and family considerations, and personal environmental preferences (Goldstein and Goldstein, 1996). This means, in turn, that the composition of the Conservative population in different regions varies because of selective migration and the impact of duration of residence.

The important role that migration has played in the development of the Conservative communities in the South and the West is evident from data on lifetime migration. Whereas about one-fifth of the Conservative Jews living in the Northeast and Midwest were born in the same communities in which they were living in 1990 (Table 25), this was true of only 6 percent of the Conservative Jews in the South and 7 percent of those in the West. Over three-fourths of Conservative

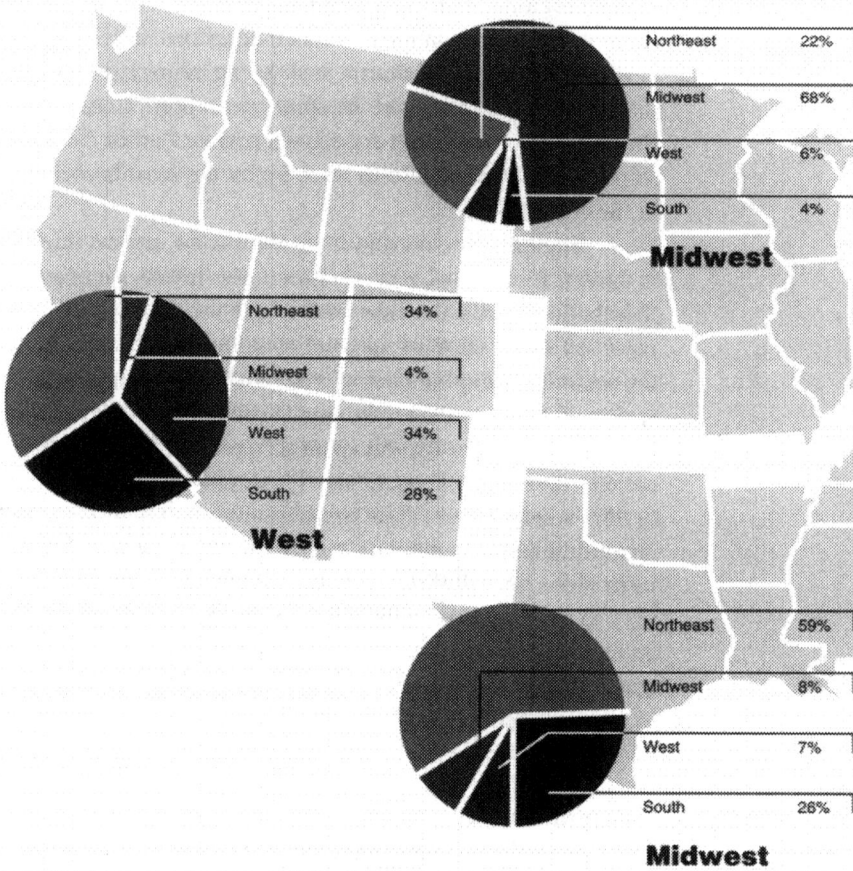

Figure 12 Region of Birth of Adult Conservative Jews, by Region of Current Residence

Midwest

Northeast	22%
Midwest	68%
West	6%
South	4%

West

Northeast	34%
Midwest	4%
West	34%
South	28%

Midwest

Northeast	59%
Midwest	8%
West	7%
South	26%

Jews living in the South and two-thirds of those in the West were born in a state different from the one in which they resided in 1990. In fact, most of these migrants were born in a different region. Many fewer Conservative Jews were interstate lifetime migrants in the Northeast (29 percent) and Midwest (37 percent). Compared to the South and the West, among the populations living in the older regions of Jewish settlement in 1990, much more of the lifetime movement involved changes in residence among communities within the state rather than between states. For all regions, the proportion of lifetime migration from overseas was low (8-11 percent), reflecting the decline in the number of foreign-born Jews as many of the immigrants of the early 1900s die.

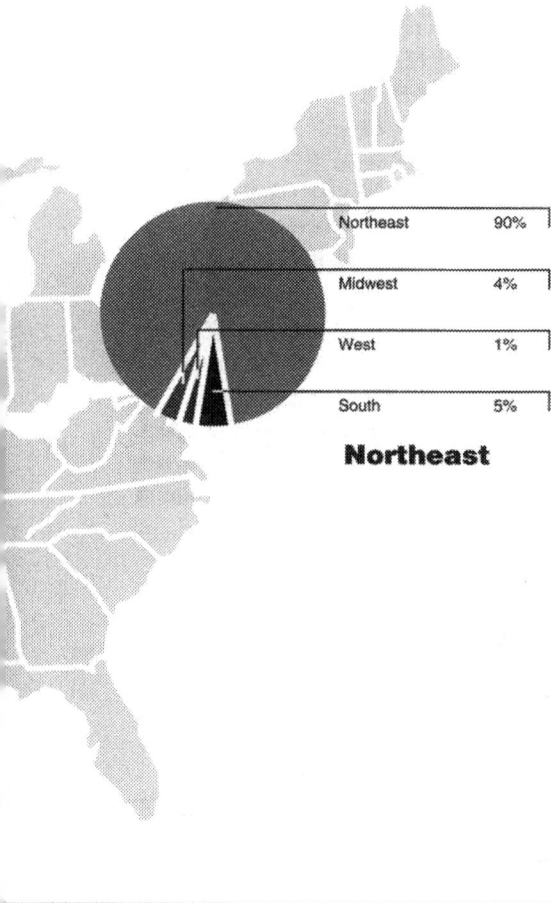

Northeast	90%
Midwest	4%
West	1%
South	5%

Northeast

Because interregional migration has been such a key factor in the changing national distribution of Conservative Jewry, it is important to identify what the specific nature of the interregional exchange has been. Information for lifetime migration for all adult American-born Conservative Jews (Table 25) shows that, for each region, the single largest group of residents were those living within the region of birth. In the Northeast and the South almost two-thirds lived within the same region, but in the Midwest only four in ten did so. In the West, over seven in ten had remained within their region of birth, reflecting its younger population and the popularity of the region not only to in-migrants but also to those born there. Clearly, by 1990 the Midwest had the lowest retention rate and the West the highest.

At the same time, regional destinations among Conservative Jews varied, depending on region of birth. This is reflected in the origins of the Conservative population living in the different regions (Figure 12). Nine-in-ten adults living in the Northeast in 1990 were born in the region, and almost seven-in-ten residents of the Midwest were from states in the same region. By contrast, attesting to the popularity of the South and the West as places of destination, only one-quarter of Conservative Jews in the South in 1990 had been born in that region; and an almost equally low proportion of residents in the West had been born there.

Each region of the country, except the Northeast, has clearly seen a growth in their Conservative populations because of shifts from other regions; but the direction of movement has varied. The Northeast was the largest supplier of migrants to the South and the West; but a high proportion of migrants to the West also came from the Midwest. Far fewer came from the South. Only small numbers of

Conservative Jews who moved interregionally went to the Northeast.

The very high proportions of interstate migrants (many of whom changed region of residence in the process of moving) among Conservative Jews in the West and South and their significant numbers even in the Northeast and Midwest, supplemented by considerable intrastate migration, highlight the importance of geographic mobility. The disruptions associated with such movement may have a serious impact on the degree and type of integration into the local community and affect the strength of Jewish identity generally and intensity of affiliation with Conservative Jewry in particular. It may well account for some of the regional differences in rates of involvement in Jewish activities and in adherence to Jewish ritual practices.

This possibility is reinforced by the regional data on recent migration, that is, within the five-year period preceding the 1990 survey (Table 26). Again, the data point to higher rates of movement among those living in the South and the West, although the differentials are not as sharp as those for lifetime migration. In part, this pattern is due to the shorter period encompassed by the five-year migration measure. Furthermore, because communities in the South and the West have become more established, they include more residents who may themselves engage in intrastate and interstate migration.

In each region but the West, about one-in-five Conservative Jews changed their community of residence over this short period; in the West, one in four did so. These rates attest to the significance, both positive and negative, of mobility for the vitality of the Conservative population in each region. On the one hand, if movement is to already-established Conservative communities, it can certainly enhance the density of the Conservative population at destination and make that Conservative Jewish community more viable. At the same time, it may reduce the population at origin to a point that maintenance of infrastructure and activities becomes more difficult. And if movement is dispersed and to communities that lack any kind of Jewish infrastructure, individuals may be lost not only to the Conservative movement but also to American Jewry as a whole. For individual Jews, whether the effect is positive or negative will depend on whether they are moving to a location with greater or lesser Jewish opportunities to practice Judaism, and whether they integrate into the Jewish life of the community at destination. The situation presents challenges for both individuals and communities at origin and destination.

Interregional migration has operated as an important force in redistributing the Conservative population between 1985 and 1990 (Table 26). Between 5 and 15 percent of the 1985 residents of the varied regions had migrated to another region by 1990 (middle panel). The Northeast, the South, and the West varied minimally in their proportion of interregional migrants, between 5 percent and 6 percent, but the Midwest lost about 15 percent of its adult Conservative Jews to other regions between 1985 and 1990. These patterns parallel those revealed by the lifetime data. In comparison to the lifetime data, however, the West has a somewhat lower retention rate in recent years, more closely resembling the Northeast and the South. This may stem from the changing economic conditions in the West that lead to somewhat more movement to other areas of the country.

The interregional flows had different impacts on the four regions (lower panel). Consistent with our earlier observation, more of the movers to the Northeast were from the South than from other regions; many may have been return migrants who had earlier moved to the South. The Midwest drew most of its recent in-migrants from the Northeast, but many also came from the West. The latter were probably return migrants, since many lifetime migrants from the Midwest had migrated to the West in earlier years. Not surprisingly, the South drew the majority of its recent migrants from the Northeast and the Midwest. Consistent with lifetime patterns of movement, over half of the West's recent in-migrants originated in the Northeast.

Overall, judged by the extent and direction of both lifetime and recent interregional migration, Conservative Jewry has participated extensively in the national redistribution of American Jewry as a whole. As a result, regional differences in demographic characteristics and in the character of Jewish identity take on added significance in understanding Conservative Jewry and the challenges it faces (cf., Wertheimer and Keysar, 1997).

Metropolitan Residence
One facet in the redistribution process in which Jews have widely participated has been movement out of central cities to suburbs and more outlying parts of the metropolitan areas or even beyond them. Does the metropolitan residence pattern of Conservative Jews vary regionally? In all regions, the great majority of Conservative Jews (95-96 percent) live within metropolitan areas (Table 27).

Residential patterns within metropolitan areas vary considerably, however. The Midwest and the South had the highest concentration of Conservative Jews in the central cities of metropolitan areas, about two-thirds. The Northeast and the West closely resembled each other in having less than half of all their Conservative Jews living in central cities. The suburbanization movement and the changing ethnic-racial composition of core cities undoubtedly account for this low percentage in the older cities of the Northeast. The structure of metropolitan areas in the West helps to account for the lower percentage of Conservative Jews who are central city residents, compared to the South and the Midwest.

Conversely, suburban living was most popular for Conservative Jews in the West, where half lived outside the central cities but within metropolitan areas. Almost as many in the Northeast did so, compared to only 29 percent of those in the Midwest and one-third of those in the South. These varied regional patterns of metropolitan residence have serious implications for the location of infrastructure, such as synagogues and day schools, associated with Conservative Judaism and with the larger Jewish community. In particular, this distribution must be taken into account in programming and planning for future development, drawing on the experience of those communities that have already undergone significant shifts in their centers of population.

Regional Differences in Age Composition
Just as the various denominations differ in their age structure, so, too, do the Conservative populations of the various regions (Table 28). Whereas the median age for all Conservative Jews is 40.1, it is above that in the Northeast (42.5), below that in the Midwest (36.6) and the West (36.8), and approximately the same in the South. These differentials are the result of quite different age distributions in the four regions. The Midwest and the West each has a disproportionately large number of children below age 18 and relatively fewer in the age groups 45 and over. The South has a dearth of persons aged 45-64 but a much higher percentage of elderly consistent with its attraction for retirees. The Northeast's relatively high concentration of persons aged 45-64 helps to account for its higher median age. The Northeast's and the Midwest's lower-than-average percentage of elderly may be the result of the movement of many retirees to the South.

These variations in the age profiles of the four regions suggest that approaches to planning and programming for Conservative communities may have to vary considerably to take account of age composition. More activities in the Midwest and West will have to cater to younger constituencies than in the Northeast and South.

Socioeconomic Differences Among Regions
Life Cycle. The information on household composition reinforces the foregoing evidence on the extent of regional differences in age composition. While the proportion of one-person units under age 45 varies quite narrowly across regions, the proportion of one-person units aged 45 and over is much higher in the Northeast and South than in the West and the Midwest (Table 29). The most common type unit in all regions consists of two or more adults only, but even here the

proportion ranges from one-third in the Northeast and the South to 46 percent in the Midwest. The West and the Midwest have the highest proportion of units consisting of parent(s) and children under age 15, and the Northeast out-ranks all other regions in the proportion of parental units containing children aged 15 and over. These regional variations are in part due to regional differences in age composition, life styles, family values, and housing, but other factors undoubtedly contribute to the variations. From a community perspective, it is important that the differences be recognized and taken into account in planning services and activities.

Marital Status. To a considerable degree, regional differences among Conservative Jews in marital status reflect those in age composition. Both the Northeast and the South have a high percentage of widowed. The South is outstanding in its high proportion of divorced/separated persons, suggesting that marital disruptions, whether by death or divorce/separation, characterize far more of the Conservative Jews in the South than in any other region. The South and the West have comparatively fewer who have never been married. By contrast, a relatively high proportion of Conservative adults in the Northeast and Midwest are still single.

The high proportion of adults not currently married in each region, ranging from slightly over one-third in the Midwest and the West to almost half of those in the Northeast and the South, points to the importance of recognizing regional variations in marital status and family composition within the Conservative Jewish population. Moreover, even within the large, currently nonmarried segment of the population, the specific marital status varies greatly by region.

Intermarriage. Among the most striking regional differences are patterns of intermarriage. With 21 percent of Conservative Jews in a mixed marriage nationally, the Northeast closely follows the national pattern. In the Midwest and the South, the levels of mixed marriages are much lower; in the South, this is partly because of the concentration of older persons in that region. In the West, mixed marriage rates are far above the national level, with about one-in-three in such unions. By contrast, the highest rates of conversionary marriages are in the Midwest and the South. These sharp regional differences are the result of a combination of factors, such as age, migration status, and education, or the more general regional characteristics, including traditional vs. liberal outlook and life styles.

Education. Surprisingly, the educational composition of Conservative Jews varies greatly by region and not in ways that might be expected. Given the large concentrations of both educational institutions and high-tech industries in the Northeast and the West, we expected these regions to have the highest percentage of Conservative

Jews with graduate/professional education. In fact, the proportion who went beyond an undergraduate college degree is highest in the Midwest and at a lower level in the other three regions. The preponderance of Conservative Jews in the Northeast and the West with only one to four years of college education suggests that graduate education is not a prerequisite for the types of careers undertaken in these regions. Reversing the pattern of differentials noted for graduate studies, the Midwest has the lowest proportion of adults with no more than a high school education. Some of these regional variations reflect differential age composition and the associated concentrations of foreign-born. Some are the result of selective out- and in-migration. Other factors, including career opportunities, also help explain the regional differences.

Occupation. [9] Strong regional differences characterize the occupational composition of the Conservative Jewish population. In part, these reflect educational differences, but they are also related to factors in the regional economies.

Among males, the proportion of managers shows the widest regional variation of any occupational group, ranging from 24 percent in the Northeast to only 5 percent in the South. Quite likely, more men in the Northeast have retained management of their own businesses enterprises that may well have been founded by immigrant ancestors while others may hold managerial level positions in the many financial and service industries located in the Northeast. Lower white collar and blue collar positions are prominent among men in the South, perhaps because older persons are able to fill such less demanding positions upon retirement. The Midwest has the highest percentages of professionals.

The regional occupational profiles for women are quite different. The Midwest (in striking contrast to the pattern for men) has the lowest percentage of professionals, but, by far, the highest percentage of managers among women. Women in each region have high concentrations in the clerical/sales positions, especially in the South. Fewer women than men are blue collar workers, except in the West.

These regional differences in occupational distributions are often striking, and the differences between men's and women's occupational patterns are strong. They particularly suggest the unique characteristics of the Conservative Jewish population of the South, where a much larger proportion are employed in lower-status occupations and, therefore, are also likely to have more constrained

---

9. As was done in our previous analysis of occupation, the data are restricted to those in the labor force at the time of the survey and are presented separately for men and women.

financial resources. In each of the other regions, Conservative Jewish men are overwhelmingly in high occupational positions; women are professionals or managers to a somewhat lesser extent. Taken together with their high educational achievements, the population's occupational status in each region suggests not only that programming must be at a suitable level of sophistication, but also that the limited time available for volunteering must be channeled into appropriate types of activities.

Regional Differences in Indicators of Jewish Identity
Given regional differentials in socioeconomic characteristics, we expect to find differences in indicators of Jewish identity as well. The high levels of migration in the South and the West may have a particularly strong impact on involvement with Jewish institutions and organizations. Levels of mixed marriage are also closely related to strength of Jewish identity; and, as we have seen, intermarriage patterns differ sharply among regions. We expect that the West will have especially low scores on indicators of strength of Jewish identity and that the Northeast will have a much higher score. Our assumptions are partially supported by the data.

Jewish Education. Some regional differences exist in the extent of Jewish education of Conservative Jews (Table 30). The greatest regional differences are among those having no or only a low level of Jewish education, with the West clearly marked as the region having the greatest proportion of Conservative Jews in these categories. As the region with the highest density of Jewish population and Jewish institutions, the Northeast had the lowest percentage of Conservative Jews with no Jewish education. Regional differences in the percentage with a high level of Jewish education are minimal. Some of the overall regional difference may be due to the availability of Jewish educational facilities at the time the NJPS-1990 respondents were of school age. The West may also have attracted more Jews who, while identifying as Conservative in 1990, were raised as secular Jews and, therefore, received minimal childhood Jewish education. Despite these regional variations, concerns about the Conservative population's knowledge about Judaism are relevant in each region and need to be addressed.

Ritual Practices. Very clear regional differences appear in scores on the Ritual Scale (Figure 13). Conservative Jews in the Northeast and Midwest are far more traditional in their observances than those in the South and the West. For example, the percentage in the highest-observance category declines from 30 percent in the Northeast to only 16 percent in the West. Conversely, the proportion with either no practices or only a low score is almost twice as high in the South and the West than in the Northeast and the Midwest.

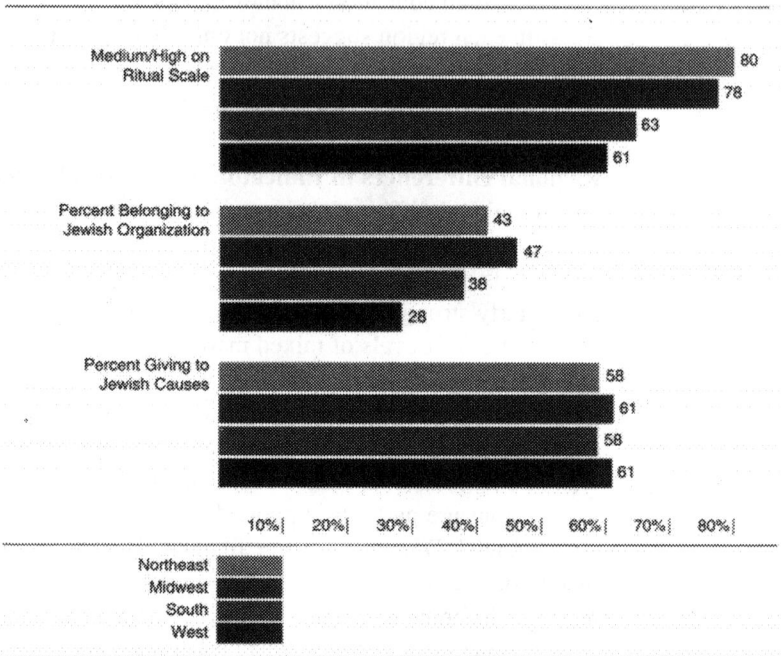

Figure 13 Selected Jewish Identificational Characteristics of Adult Conservative Jews, by Region

Apparently, the regions into which Jews have moved in large numbers in recent decades are the ones with relatively fewer observant Conservative Jews. Whether this is the result of selective in-migration of the less observant or is due to assimilation of preexisting norms in the regions of destination cannot be ascertained here. It is clear, however, that if judged by practice, Conservative Jews living in the West, and to a lesser extent those in the South, differ sharply in their adherence to Conservative practices from those in the Northeast and the Midwest. Thus, although a majority of Conservatives in all regions reported medium or high levels of ritual practices, the regional differences are important indicators of the kinds of questions that must be raised about national and regional planning for the Conservative movement.

Involvement in the Jewish Community. If our focus shifts from ritual practices to involvement in the formal structure of the Jewish community as indicators of Jewish identity, regional variations are again clearly apparent, but not entirely in the expected patterns. Membership in Jewish organizations and, especially, involvement in voluntarism in Jewish activities are highest in the Midwest. Conservative Jews in the Northeast have quite similar levels of membership but much lower levels of voluntarism. Consistent with our findings on ritual practices, those living in the South and the West have low levels of involvement. Conservative Jews living in the West are conspicuously less involved in Jewish volunteer activity only 16 percent, compared to 46 percent in the Midwest.

Regional differences are greatly narrowed when we consider contributions to Jewish causes. In fact, Jews in the West have the highest level of giving. Whether these patterns indicate generally equal success by fund raising agencies in contacting the Jewish population and convincing them to make contributions, or whether, instead, contributing is seen as a substitute for more personal involvement cannot be ascertained from the available data. It is an issue that warrants exploration, especially since, in comparison to giving to Jewish causes, the level of involvement in organizations and volunteer activity is so low in all regions.

Visits to Israel. Ties to Israel (as measured by ever visiting) are considered an important aspect of Jewish identity. Again, considerable regional variations exist in the percentage who have ever visited Israel. Conservative Jews in the South report the highest level of visits (43 percent). The population in the South is older than that of other regions; more have, therefore, had time to undertake visits, possibly after retirement. The South's older age composition also means that more of its residents directly remember the creation of the State of Israel and the subsequent wars, so that they are more likely to have developed emotional attachments to that country. By contrast, in the West, just under one-third of Conservative Jews have ever visited Israel. This may partially reflect the West's younger population, but may also be related to the greater costs of flying from the West to Israel than from other regions.

Jewish Milieu. As we have observed, many of the differences among the regions in the characteristics and behavior of Conservative Jews may be the result of a variety of factors in both the general and Jewish communities. One measure of the Jewish community context is provided by the Jewish Milieu Score,[10] which is affected by the community context and perhaps even more by the strength of an individual's ties to the Jewish community.

The Jewish milieu in which Conservative Jews function varies greatly by region. The greatest proportion of Conservative Jews with a high Jewish Milieu Score live in the Northeast and the South. These are areas of high density housing (apartments and condominiums) where Jews can easily cluster; retirees in the South are particularly likely to do so. By contrast, only 12 percent of those in the West have a high score; those in the Midwest are intermediate, with almost one-

---

10. The Jewish Milieu Score incorporates number of Jewish friends, Jewish density of neighborhood, and importance of living in a Jewish neighborhood. See p.54 for further details.

third having a high score. Conversely, a much higher percentage in the West than in the other regions scored low on Jewish milieu. While gross statistics such as these mask local differences, the regional differences are in themselves striking and reinforce the pattern of lower levels of Jewish identification in the West than in the other regions.

Synagogue Membership. Data discussed earlier showed substantial regional differences in levels of synagogue membership; Conservative Jews in the Northeast and the Midwest had much higher rates of affiliation than did those in the South and the West. Earlier in this chapter, the five-year migration statistics indicated that a higher proportion of the adults living in the South and the West are interstate migrants than is true of the Northeast and the West. To what extent are these two patterns related? Are the interstate migrants to the South and the West adopting the synagogue membership patterns of the nonmigrant Conservative Jews, or is mobility the explanation for the lower levels of membership characterizing these two regions? Concurrent attention to membership levels by migration status for Conservative Jews in each of the regions provides some insights into these questions. (Data not shown in tables.)

Just over half of the nonmigrants (persons living in the same location in 1990 as in 1985) in the Northeast and the Midwest belong to synagogues, but only one-third of those living in the South and West do. This differential suggests that factors associated with the characteristics of the populations living in these regions help explain regional variations. A similar pattern in levels of membership characterizes the intrastate movers in the three regions. Intrastate Conservative movers in the Northeast have a high level of membership; those in the South and the West have a much lower level, closely resembling the nonmigrants. This reinforces the basic regional differentials.

A different pattern emerges, however, for the interstate migrants. Those in the Northeast have a lower rate of affiliation than the nonmigrants in the region, suggesting that migration for them is either disruptive of institutional ties and/or that the migrants are selective of persons with low affiliation, who continue to maintain those lower levels. For Conservative Jewish interstate migrants in the South, however, the levels of synagogue affiliation are higher than for the nonmigrants in the region. Since a disproportional number of these migrants are retirees moving from the Northeast and Midwest, their affiliation behavior may be influenced by the higher levels that characterize their regions of origin, even though the absolute affiliation level of these migrants is somewhat below that of Conservative Jews at origin. Alternatively, for the elderly migrants, affiliation may serve as a way to integrate into the social and religious life at destination.

For interstate migrants to the West, by contrast, the rate of affiliation is especially low, only 23 percent, well below the levels both in other regions and among the non-migrants in the West. As for migrants to the Northeast, migration itself may, therefore, be disruptive of affiliation. Data suggest that for both the Northeast and the West, longer residence does attenuate the migrant/nonmigrant differentials.

* * * * *

Clearly, the character of the Conservative populations living in the four regions varies. In general, the Conservative Jews of the Northeast and the Midwest are more traditional in their orientation and more strongly identified with the Jewish community than are those in the South and the West. Thus, in the West, a Jewish milieu is of much less importance than in the other regions, and intermarriage levels are strikingly higher. By contrast, Jewish organizational membership and voluntarism in Jewish activities are exceptionally high in the Midwest. The one exception to these strong regional patterns is the similar percentage in each region contributing to Jewish causes.

The overall regional differences are to a large extent reflected in the individual communities located within the respective regions. Communities in the eastern part of the country (with some exceptions) encompassed Conservative populations of generally similar profiles, with similar Judaic behavior and attachments. They differed from western communities that, in turn, were quite similar to each other.

Several explanations may account for the regional differences. Selective migration may dispose persons with certain characteristics and types of Jewish identity to move to one location instead of another. The individuals themselves would, thereby, influence the character of the community in which they lived. Conversely, the communities to which migrants come have a particular kind of ambience that may or may not be conducive to strong Jewish identification and involvement. The community would thus help to shape the behavior of its residents. The available data do not allow us to distinguish the factors influencing behavior, but a combination of both individual and community characteristics most likely contribute to a full explanation.

As a result of migration and resettlement, the Conservative Jewish population has been dramatically redistributed across the United States, and migration has become an important factor influencing the extent of individuals' integration into Jewish communal life. The redistribution of population, in the longer run, has served not to homogenize the patterns among regions but rather to reinforce the differentials. This provides a challenge to institutions interested in raising levels of synagogue affiliation and enhancing other forms of

Judaic practices and behavior. To assume that the same "formula" will work across the nation overlooks what appears to be underlying regional differences.

VI. Conservative Jewry: A Fluid Population

Conservative Jewry in the United States is a dynamic population in a constant state of change. Its general socioeconomic and Jewish identificational characteristics vary by age and region of residence. Moreover, its very size fluctuates as a result of both natural forces (births and deaths) and social change processes.

Changing fertility levels create conditions of faster or slower growth over the generations. In addition, the age structure of the population affects not only the overall birth rate but also the death rate; an older population is characterized by more deaths than births. In the closing decades of the twentieth century, for example, the birth rate of Jewish Americans has probably been inadequate to compensate for the high death rate associated with an aging population.

Unfortunately, the absence of any direct information on religious identity on birth and death records nationwide prevents easy assessment of the role of natural increase on changes in the size of either the Jewish population as a whole or particular denominations. Data from NJPS-1990 and Jewish community surveys on number of children born do allow limited insights on denominational differentials in fertility, but the absence of comparable information on deaths does not permit assessment of natural change.

Natural change is only one set of factors that can account for denominational growth, stability, or decline. More important perhaps is the extent to which children reared in a particular denomination by their parent(s) remain identified with that denomination as adults, switch to another denomination, become nondenominational, or in some instances, forego their Jewish identity. Long-term trends among Jewish Americans have seen a decline in the attractiveness of more traditional ideologies and practices, with a concomitant shift away from Orthodox toward Reform Judaism. Such shifting in response to personal preferences is a major mechanism by which particular denominations grow or decline. Other factors contributing to denominational switching include marriage between persons raised in different denominations, becoming a Jew by choice, and migration to areas where institutions associated with the preferred denomination are not available. Social pressures by peers, colleagues, family, and neighbors may also contribute to denominational switching. Departures from the Jewish fold to adopt the non-Jewish religion of a spouse in the case of mixed marriages may also impinge on the size of particular denominations.

71

The Magnitude and Direction of Changes

The availability in NJPS-1990 of information about the respondent's current denominational preference, as well as the denomination in which the respondents were raised, allows some evaluation of changes in denominational affiliation within the lifetime of the respondent. This information is, of course, limited to adult Jews who were living in 1990. Moreover, denomination-raised refers to a wide time range, since respondents cover a large age span. While this can be partially controlled by attention to broad age differences, the information still does not present a fully accurate cross-section of the denominational affiliation of Jews at any given time in the past. Within these limitations, the data point to substantial changes in the denominational identity of currently Conservative Jews.

Earlier analysis has shown that, in 1990, 36 percent of adult Jewish Americans identify as Conservative Jews. Conservative Jewry was, thus, the second largest denomination, exceeded slightly by Reform Jews, who accounted for 38 percent. Constituting a small minority in 1990 were the Orthodox, at only 6 percent. In fact, the Orthodox were slightly outnumbered by both the 10 percent who regarded themselves as Just Jewish and the 9 percent classified as Other. Reconstructionist Jews were only a little more than 1 percent of all Jews.

The largest proportion of adult core Jews were raised as Conservative (34 percent); just under one-quarter were raised as Reform, and approximately another one-quarter as Orthodox (Table 31). Only 8 percent reported being raised as Just Jewish, 6 percent as Other, and 3 percent as non-Jews.[11] A comparison of the denominational profile of adult Jews in 1990 with the denomination in which they were raised as children shows that the proportion of Conservative Jews among all American Jews has changed minimally, remaining just over one-third of the total. By contrast, the Orthodox population experienced a sharp decline, while the proportion of Reform Jews increased. Since this realignment occurred within the lifetime of the surveyed individuals, it points to substantial shifting in denominational identity. In fact, the relative stability in the proportion that Conservative Jews constitute of the total is misleading since it is the end result of specific individuals switching in and out of the denomination, with the gains and losses largely canceling each other out.

The degree of switching can be understood better by examining the denominations in which those defining themselves as Conservative in 1990 were raised. Only about six-in-ten currently Conservative Jews were also raised in that denomination, and the situation is very similar

---

11. The percentage raised as non-Jews is well below the intermarriage rate because these data are based on respondents, and the survey preferred respondents who were identified currently as Jewish.

for Reform Jewry. Among the currently Orthodox Jews, however, the large majority (89 percent) had been raised in that denomination. These data thus point to the importance of denominational switching in the growth of the Conservative and Reform movements. Where did the switchers to Conservative Judaism come from and where did those who left the movement go?

In total, about 1,645,000 adults indicated that they had been raised as Conservative Jews (Table 32). Of these, 916,800, almost six in ten, still identified with Conservative Judaism in 1990. Some 727,900 adults switched to another denomination or to another religion. The largest number who switched out of Conservative Judaism (429,100) became Reform Jews (Figure 14). Another 11 percent of the switchers from Conservative Judaism became Just Jewish, and 10 percent identified as Other. Only 2 percent moved in the more traditional direction, to Orthodox Judaism. About 4 percent became Reconstructionist Jews. Especially striking is the 13 percent of out-switchers who identified as Protestant or Catholic.

Figure 14 **Denominational Flows Into and Out of Conservative Judaism**

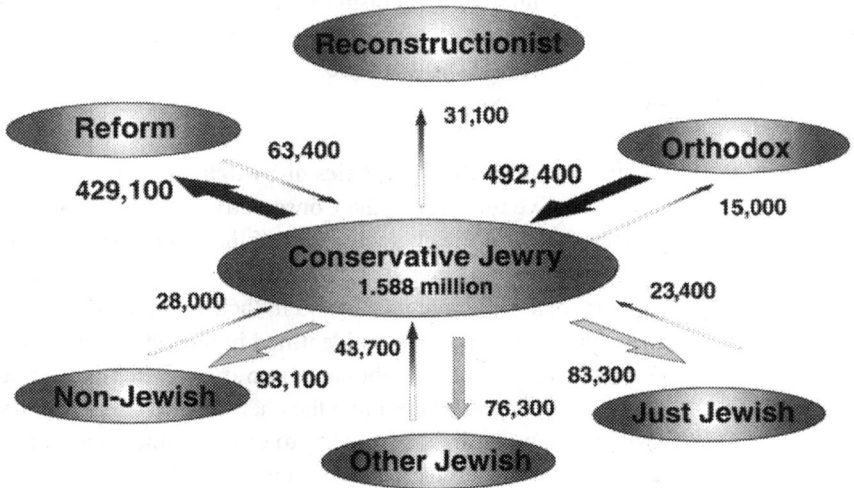

Of the estimated 650,900 adult Conservative Jews who were not raised in this denomination, the greatest number (some 492,400) had an Orthodox upbringing, thus going from a more to a somewhat less traditional orientation. Only 10 percent were drawn from Reform Judaism. The small remainder were drawn from those indicating a

Just Jewish or non-Jewish upbringing and from the heterogeneous other group.

Thus, just as Conservative Jewry attracted the largest number from the more traditional Orthodox adherents, it lost the greatest number to the less traditional Reform movement, reflecting the general shift of American Jewry from more to less traditional religious orientations and practices. The large exodus from the movement means that the substantial gains made from Orthodox Judaism were canceled out: Conservative Judaism actually experienced a net loss of an estimated 77,000 persons over the course of the lifetime of the respondents encompassed in NJPS-1990, largely to the Reform movement. This small net loss, resulting from a very high volume of switching, explains why the proportion of Conservative Jews in the total Jewish American population has remained quite stable at just over one-third.

In view of the small pool of Orthodox population in the United States in 1990, and because a substantial part of that pool either is strongly committed to Orthodox Judaism or is elderly, the Conservative movement can no longer look to Orthodox Jewry as a source of replenishment of the losses it sustains to denominations on its left. Rather, to remain stable and, especially, to grow, it must develop an internal dynamism to retain those raised as Conservative Jews and to attract Reform and Reconstructionist Jews and/or those not currently identified with a denomination. Failure to do so will lead to declining numbers.

Socioeconomic Characteristics of Switchers

The extensive turnover in the Conservative population argues for better understanding of the characteristics of those who left the movement as well as those who entered it. We assume that these two groups differ in their socioeconomic profile and in their religious practices, and that the Conservative population identified in the 1990 survey is quite different from what it might have been if no switching had occurred. Our assessment will determine the characteristics of stayers and switchers, and how those moving to or from other denominations differ from or resemble both each other and those who were raised and remain Conservative. In undertaking this evaluation, we recognize that the characteristics refer to 1990, the year of the survey, and do not reflect conditions at the time the switching occurred. In fact, we do not know when the actual change in denominational identity took place or under what circumstances; we have information only on denomination in which the respondent was raised and denomination at the time of the survey.[12]

Age. The 1990 age profile of persons raised as Orthodox Jews who switched to Conservative Judaism is considerably older than that of Conservative stayers (Table 33). Over half of the Orthodox switchers were aged 65 and over in 1990, and another 24 percent were aged 45-64 compared to only 42 percent of stayers in these two age groups combined. This pattern suggests that switching from Orthodox to Conservative Judaism occurred some time ago. Much of it may have involved the children of immigrants who were raised in the traditions of their parents, but who were attracted to the more modern and "American" style of the Conservative movement once they formed their own households.

By contrast, the numerically smaller group of switchers from Reform to Conservative Judaism were much younger than the Orthodox switchers and even somewhat younger than the Conservative stayers; only 19 percent were elderly. Over four in ten were under age 35 compared to only 9 percent of the Orthodox switchers and 32 percent of the Conservative stayers. Conservative Judaism appears to have been more attractive in recent years to younger Reform Jews. By contrast, 70-80 percent of those switching from Just Jewish and from the Other category were in the 35-64 age range, compared to just under half of those who remained Conservative.

How do these age profiles compare with those who left the Conservative movement? Too few shifted to Orthodox Judaism to allow valid statistical comparisons. Of those who became Reform Jews, the proportion of aged closely resembled the stayers. The greatest difference characterized those aged 45-64, who constituted 31 percent of the switchers to Reform Judaism but only 22 percent of the stayers. On average, the large number of switchers from Conservative to Reform Judaism were older than the much smaller number coming from the Reform movement. Possibly, like the Orthodox Jews who became Conservative, many of the Conservative Jews who switched to Reform Judaism did so early in adulthood. However, a considerable portion of the switching may have occurred in later life as older Conservative Jews followed their own children and grandchildren to Reform temples.

By contrast, far fewer of the switchers to Reconstructionism or to Just Jewish were either elderly or middle-aged; most were concentrated in the 25-44 age range. Their loss to the Conservative movement, especially if the trend accelerates, has serious implications, both because the adults themselves may create a serious gap in support and leadership and because their children may be lost to Conservative Jewry. Those shifting into the Other category were somewhat older than the previously mentioned two groups.

---

12 Summary data showing the characteristics of the in- and out-switchers are presented in Appendix Table C.

Still different were those who were raised as Conservative Jews but who regarded themselves as non-Jewish by the time of the survey. Over 10 percent were elderly, and more than half were between ages 35 and 64. Perhaps most significant is that just over one-third were between ages 18 and 34, indicating that a substantial proportion of those lost to Conservative Judaism altogether were young persons. In this respect, they closely resemble those who left Conservative Judaism to become Just Jewish. The high concentration of switchers out of Judaism in this younger group may be associated with mixed marriages in which the Jewish partner chose to adopt the religion of the non-Jewish spouse or to forego any religious identity.

On balance, the cumulative effect of switching in and out of Conservative Judaism is an aging of the Conservative population. Almost three times as many of all those who joined than of those who left were, by 1990, elderly. More of those who left than who joined were in each of the age groups under age 65; but the differences were especially great among those under age 45 and even more so among those aged 18-24.

Life-cycle Stage. Family life-cycle stage is highly correlated with age of respondent. Not surprisingly, therefore, a disproportionately large number of the Orthodox switchers to Conservative Judaism in 1990 were either members of adults-only units or persons aged 45 and over living by themselves. Far more of the Conservative stayers and switchers from Reform to Conservative Judaism than of Orthodox switchers had children at home. Both the Just Jewish and the Other group of in-switchers had far more units with children in the household than did either the stayers or those switching from Orthodox or Reform Judaism.

By contrast, those Conservative Jews who switched to Reform Judaism quite closely resembled the Conservative stayers, although fewer were young one-person units and more lived in adults-only households. Again, as a function of their younger average age, far more switchers from Conservative to Reconstructionist Judaism were younger persons living by themselves, as couples, or in units with young children. So, too, a disproportional number of those shifting to Just Jewish and to Other were either in adults-only units or in units with young children. Those raised as Conservative Jews who became non-Jewish were heavily concentrated in units with children. The low proportion of one-person units among those who became non-Jews supports the thesis that marriage is an important factor in accounting for this particular change.

While these data refer to life-cycle stage in 1990 rather than at the time of switching, they do point to selective in- and out-movement to and from Conservative Judaism of persons with different family situations. On balance, the movement has lost more persons at early stages of the life cycle and gained more who in 1990 lived in adults-only units or were older persons living alone.

Marital Status. Marital status is also closely related to age. Older populations include more widowed persons; more of the younger population have not yet married; and the middle aged are likely to be either married or separated/divorced. Not surprisingly, therefore, the Orthodox switchers to Conservative Judaism are composed disproportionately of widowed persons. The stayers, by contrast, have the highest proportion of never-married persons. The somewhat lower proportion of never-married and the very high percent of married among the switchers from Reform Judaism likely stems from a tendency of people to shift from the Reform to the Conservative movement upon marriage and child rearing. Unlike the Orthodox and Reform switchers to Conservative Judaism, far more of those shifting from both the Just Jewish and the Other category were separated/divorced. Perhaps for these groups, marital disruption leads to a greater need to identify, possibly in the interest of creating a more Judaic ambiance for children in the unit.

Among those who have left Conservative Judaism, a consistently higher-than-average proportion were married persons compared to the stayers. While we have no evidence that allows direct testing of whether the exodus occurred in association with or as a consequence of marriage and/or family formation, the pattern suggests this as likely. Lower-than-average percentages of separated/divorced and widowed are found among the switchers. In addition, among the large number of shifters from Conservative to Reform Judaism, the proportion of individuals who never married is greater than among those switching in the opposite direction. This difference suggests that those who are not married may have a greater tendency to shift to a less traditional group.

Interestingly, a disproportional number of those who had shifted to the non-Jewish group were in the separated/divorced category, and all but a minority of the others were married. The high proportion of currently and formerly married reinforces the earlier interpretation that shifting out of Judaism is probably associated with mixed marriages. That a substantial proportion are separated/divorced may indicate the instability of the marriages that involved a partner changing religious identity.

Intermarriage. To the extent that the rate of intermarriage varies among denominations (it is higher among the less traditional and lower among the more traditional), we would expect that fewer of the persons switching to Conservative Judaism from Reform Judaism and Just Jewish would be intermarried, and, conversely, that more of those switching out to Reform Judaism or Just Jewish would be intermarried. Switching to Reform Judaism might have a particularly strong appeal to the intermarried because the Reform movement recognizes Jewish patrilineal descent, allowing children of mixed marriages to be considered Jewish if they are raised Jewishly. Reform congregations have also had an active outreach program to the mixed married. We expect many of those shifting to Conservative Judaism from the Other group (which includes former non-Jews) to be Jews by choice, with many in a conversionary marriage, while a large proportion of those leaving Conservative Judaism to become Just Jewish or Other are likely to be in a mixed marriage. The data support such expectations. Again, it is important to remember that our data do not allow us to determine when the switching occurred or whether it was in conjunction with marriage.

Of those raised as Conservative Jews and still Conservative, about seven in ten were in-married. Yet, indicative of the rising levels of intermarriage, 26 percent were in mixed marriages. By contrast, far more of the switchers to Conservative Judaism were in-married. Nonetheless, 15 percent of the Orthodox in-switchers were mixed-married, suggesting that the Orthodox partners in a mixed marriage may turn to the Conservative movement because they perceive it as less halakhically rigorous and more accepting of persons who violate this strong taboo.

A very different pattern emerges for those who have switched out of Conservative Judaism. Compared to the 83 percent of joiners from Reform who were in-married, only two-thirds of those leaving Conservative Judaism to become Reform had in-married; one in four were in mixed marriages. Among those shifting to Just Jewish, the mixed marriage rate was twice as high. And almost all of those raised as Conservative Jews who indicated Other at the time of the survey were in mixed marriages. Consistent with earlier expectations, the type of marriage of those who switched from being Conservative to non-Jewish is unique; all such out-switchers were married to a non-Jewish spouse. This marriage pattern strongly suggests that for most of those who leave Conservative Judaism and become non-Jewish, the switch occurred in conjunction with marriage.

Judged by both shifts into Conservative Jewry and shifts to Reform Judaism and other less traditional categories of denominational identity, intermarriage seems to be an important variable associated with these movements. High levels of mixed marriages among Conservative Jews may thus be an important factor in leading to loss of adherents as they seek less stringent and more accepting religious environments in which to function. In addition to programs designed to reduce intermarriage, these findings point to the need for concerted efforts to make Conservative congregations more welcoming of intermarried couples. The goal should be to retain the Jewish partner in the marriage and to work toward the eventual conversion of the non-Jew. In addition, efforts need to be made to insure that the children of mixed marriages in which the wife is Jewish are raised as Jews, and that, in marriages in which the wife is non-Jewish, the children are halakhically converted to Judaism.

Generation Status. Denominational identity is correlated with generation status; more Orthodox are foreign-born, and more Reform have all four of their grandparents born in the United States. Conservative Jews are intermediary. Given this pattern of generational variations, we expect that persons who join Conservative Jewry from Orthodox Judaism would be closer to their immigrant roots than would be switchers from Reform Judaism and even Conservative stayers. Conversely, more of those leaving Conservative Judaism for less traditional groups would more likely be "more American."

The data generally support such a thesis. Whereas three-fourths of all those switching in had no grandparents who were American-born, this was true of only 9 percent of those switching out. Almost two-thirds of the latter had all four grandparents born in the United States, compared to only 12 percent of the in-switchers.

Of the large number raised as Orthodox Jews who switched to Conservative Judaism, nine in ten had no American-born grandparents. In this respect, they were more like the Orthodox group of origin than the Conservative group to which they shifted. While a comparatively small number of Reform Jews joined Conservative Judaism, they closely resembled the profile of the Conservative stayers. Understandably, a majority of the Other group who switched had all four grandparents American-born, undoubtedly because some were previously non-Jewish.

Quite a different pattern characterizes those who switched out of the Conservative movement. With the sole exception of those shifting to Other or identifying as non-Jewish, a large majority were persons with all four grandparents born in the United States. Generation status is, thus, a key factor in accounting for the loss of persons raised as Conservative Jews to less traditional denominations or to the nondenominational categories.

Overall, the cumulative net impact of switching has been to produce a Conservative Jewry that is heavily first- and second-generation. Therefore, in the absence of changes that would reverse the pattern of switching and make Conservative Judaism more attractive to third- and higher-generation Americans, Conservative Jewry runs the risk of continuing to lose members.

Educational and Occupational Composition. Is the shift into and from Conservative Jewry selective of persons in different social classes as indexed by education and occupation? It depends on the denominational identity of the switchers and the direction of the change. Probably reflecting a combination of their older age and generational composition, relatively more of the Orthodox switchers to Conservative Jewry than of the stayers had no more than a high school education; and, conversely, fewer had either a college or postgraduate education. The Just Jewish switchers had a similar educational profile. By contrast, the switchers from Reform Judaism were heavily concentrated in the college-educated category, while the switchers from Other included a disproportional number who had undertaken graduate studies. Overall, therefore, attracting switchers from Reform Judaism and the Other group compensated somewhat for the lower average educational level of Orthodox switchers to Conservative Judaism.

The losses to the Reform movement and other groups had the reverse effect. The great majority of those who left Conservative Jewry to identify as Reform or Reconstructionist Jews had at least a college education. Moreover, within the college-educated, a large majority of the Reconstructionist Jews had some graduate/professional studies. The switchers from Conservative Judaism to Just Jewish and Other also were predominantly college-educated. Among the out-switchers, only those who became non-Jewish included very few with a postgraduate education and a large proportion with no more than a high school education.

On balance, particularly because of the large stream of switchers to Reform Judaism, denominational switching somewhat lowered the overall educational profile of Conservative Jewry; while three-fourths of all out-switchers had some college education, this was true of only two-thirds of those becoming Conservative Jews. In part, this pattern is a function of when the switching occurred. Most of the shift from Orthodox to Conservative Jewry took place several decades ago, when the general educational level, especially among the immigrant generation, was lower than in the 1980s. The shift out of Conservative Judaism likely occurred more recently and involved younger Jews with higher levels of education.

A somewhat different pattern emerges from the comparative profiles of the occupational composition of switchers and stayers.[13] The Orthodox shifters into Conservative Judaism generally have quite similar proportions of professionals and managerial persons as the Conservative stayers but more lower white-collar workers. By contrast, those raised as Reform Jews who became Conservative were

---

13. The comparison here as earlier is restricted to persons in the labor force at the time of the survey. The data are not disaggregated by sex because of the limited number of cases.

more concentrated in the professional group and much more heavily in the clerical/sales category. Switchers from Other were even more heavily concentrated in clerical/sales and consequently underrepresented in the professional and blue collar categories. Thus, the occupational composition of the switchers varied by denominational origin, but the differences were not as great as those characterizing education. Switching into the Conservative movement, therefore, did not sharply alter the occupational composition.

Moreover, those switching out of Conservative Judaism to the Reform movement were quite similarly distributed as the Orthodox Jews who had switched in. Since those raised as Orthodox Jews constituted the largest proportion of Conservative joiners and the out-switchers to Reform Judaism the largest groups of leavers, their close similarity in occupational composition largely canceled out any impact of leaving and joining, so that the overall occupational profile of Conservative Jewry was not greatly altered.

Region of Residence. More Conservative Jews in the United States live in the Northeast than in any other region. Is this pattern replicated among both stayers and switchers? The regional distribution of those Conservative Jews with an Orthodox origin very closely resembles that of the stayers, with both groups largely concentrated in the Northeast, followed by a secondary, but substantially smaller, concentration in the South. Fewer of those switching to Conservative from Reform Judaism lived in the Northeast, and they were almost equally matched by the number living in the South. The Midwest and the West each accounted for about 15 percent of all the Reform switchers. Relatively more Just Jewish and the Other who had shifted to Conservative Judaism lived in the West. The net impact of the regional distribution of switchers to Conservative Judaism has been to make the Conservative population more widely distributed across the United States.

Of those who left the Conservative movement, those joining the Reform movement are regionally distributed in virtually the same pattern as the stayers, suggesting that region of residence per se is not a major determinant of switching to Reform Judaism. Like the stayers, almost half of those switching to Reconstructionist Judaism and to being Just Jewish lived in the Northeast, but a much more substantial proportion lived in the West; far fewer resided in the South. The most exceptional regional distribution characterized those leaving Conservative Judaism for the Other group: The highest proportion by far lived in the South, and relatively fewer were in the Northeast and the West. More of the former Conservative Jews who reported no longer being Jewish were living in the Northeast; the others were almost equally distributed among the four regions.

Overall, where the in- and out-switchers lived has resulted in some change in the distribution of Conservative Jews among the regions of the United States. More of the leavers lived in the Northeast, and more of the joiners resided in the South. Thus, some of the geographic shift in the Conservative population from the Northeast to the South may stem from the differences in the regional residential patterns of the switchers.

Metropolitan Residence. Conservative stayers were heavily concentrated in metropolitan areas, with half living in the center cities. Consistent with the general residence pattern of Orthodox Jews as a whole, more of the Orthodox switchers to Conservative Judaism were city residents; and fewer lived in outer suburbs and non-metropolitan areas than did the Conservative stayers. Nonetheless, a smaller proportion of Orthodox switchers lived in center cities than did the 1990 Orthodox population as a whole; apparently many of those leaving Orthodox Judaism had a less compelling need to live in strong centers of Jewish population than those remaining Orthodox. By contrast, the Reform in-switchers were more likely to live in suburbs and more outlying areas. This same pattern in accentuated form also characterized the Just Jewish and those switching from the Other category. Thus, it is the switchers from Orthodox Judaism who have reinforced the concentration of Conservative Jews in central cities.

Of those who shifted out of Conservative Judaism, those identifying in 1990 with the Reform movement or Just Jewish had residential distributions like the Conservative stayers'. Their departure, therefore, has had little impact on the distribution of Conservative Jews within metropolitan areas and between metropolitan and nonmetropolitan areas. The much smaller number who identify with Reconstructionist Judaism were predominantly outside the center cities. Those who switched to Other or became non-Jewish were much more concentrated outside the metropolitan areas. In this sense, their marginal identity paralleled their residential pattern. Overall, more of those switchers out of Conservative Judaism than those switching in lived in the outlying parts of the metropolitan areas or in nonmetropolitan areas, so that switching has led to a somewhat greater concentration of Conservative Jewry in the central cities and inner suburbs.

Lifetime Migration. The reasons for changes in denomination undoubtedly vary considerably from individual to individual, sometimes based on changing ideological orientations, sometimes on the impact of peers, and sometimes associated with life-cycle events such as marriage. Still another factor may be geographic mobility. Movement away from locations with particular denominational institutions may lead to a change in denomination for those persons whose ties to a particular denomination are weak. For some, it may be the change in denomination that actually stimulates the move as individuals seek an environment more compatible with their religious outlook. For some, denominational identity may in fact preclude mobility, or at least limit the choice of destination. Observant Orthodox and Conservative Jews, more so than less traditional Jews, generally require relatively easy access to such facilities as kosher butchers, synagogues, Jewish schools, and mikvehs. These needs limit the communities and even the neighborhoods in which they can live. For such persons, stability rather than mobility may be the rule, so that denominational stability is often associated with geographic stability.

For the core Jewish population as a whole, switching denomination was generally found to be associated with both higher levels of migration and greater involvement in interstate and interregional movement (Goldstein and Goldstein, 1996:180-184). The most marked difference characterized those raised as Orthodox Jews; Orthodox stayers reported sharply less migration than either Orthodox out-switchers or persons in other denominations who retained their denominational identity.

Indicative of the generally high mobility levels among Conservative Jews, over eight-in-ten American-born Conservative stayers had migrated beyond their community of birth by 1990; over half were living in a different state than that in which they were born; and 36 percent were living in a different region. How did the mobility patterns of the switchers to and from Conservative Judaism compare with that of the stayers?

For Conservative Jews, the linkages between migration and denominational switching are complex, and vary depending on the direction of change and the specific denominations involved. On the whole, however, switchers to and from Conservative Judaism are more mobile than the Conservative stayers. The most notable exception is those Orthodox in-switchers who became Conservative Jews, quite possibly because their denominational change was in connection with movement out of the center cities, where Orthodox synagogues were located, to the suburbs, where many Conservative synagogues had been established. In-switchers to Conservative Judaism who did move were more likely than stayers to have moved interregionally. Those who switched out of Conservative Judaism had much more mixed patterns. For most Conservative Jews, geographic mobility, as it relates to denominational change, is undoubtedly part of a large social mobility complex that involves alterations in an array of social, economic, and contextual characteristics, among which religious concerns do not seem to play a dominant role.

Jewish Identificational Characteristics of Switchers

Household Synagogue Membership. Among all respondents who identified themselves as Conservative Jews, 46 percent reported that they or other members of their household were members of a synagogue or temple. This contrasts with only 39 percent of the Conservative stayers. Since over half of both the Orthodox and the Reform in-switchers were synagogue members, their identification as Conservative Jews has raised the overall level of synagogue membership for the Conservative group as a whole. Even the rate of the Just Jewish was slightly above that of the stayers. These data suggest, therefore, that whatever motivates the switch to Conservative Judaism involves a stronger-than-average commitment to involvement in a synagogue. The only exception is the Other group, of whom only 30 percent were members.

A different pattern characterizes those dropping out of Conservative Judaism; out-switchers have much lower rates of membership than in-switchers. Just over one-third of those shifting to Reform and Reconstructionist Judaism were members, not very different from the Conservative stayers. Far fewer of the Just Jewish, hardly any of the Other, and none of those who identify as non-Jewish belonged to a synagogue/temple.

Switching, therefore, seems to work as a filtering process with respect to synagogue/temple affiliation rates. Those who switch in are twice as affiliated as those who leave (Figure 15). The net effect is a higher level of membership. Because of the limited reservoir of Orthodox Jews who might switch to Conservative Judaism in future years, Conservative synagogue membership rates may decline, other things being equal. This needs careful monitoring.

Jewish Education. The overall Jewish educational level of Conservative Jewry has been raised by the influx of so many persons raised as Orthodox Jews. Whereas 58 percent of the stayers in Conservative Judaism had either a medium or a high level of Jewish education, almost three-fourths of those switching from Orthodoxy had such levels; and virtually all of the differential was concentrated in the high category. Only half as many of the Orthodox switchers as the Conservative stayers had no Jewish education.

Even the smaller influx from Reform Judaism brought individuals with more Jewish education than the Conservative stayers. Two-thirds had a medium or high level, but here all the differential was in the medium category. The Just Jewish switching to Conservative Judaism had levels of Jewish education very similar to those of the stayers. Only those switching from Other had less Jewish education than the stayers; 86 percent were in the none or low categories. This undoubtedly reflects the high proportion of Jews by

| Figure 15 | Selected Characteristics of Adults Moving Into and Out of Conservative Judaism |

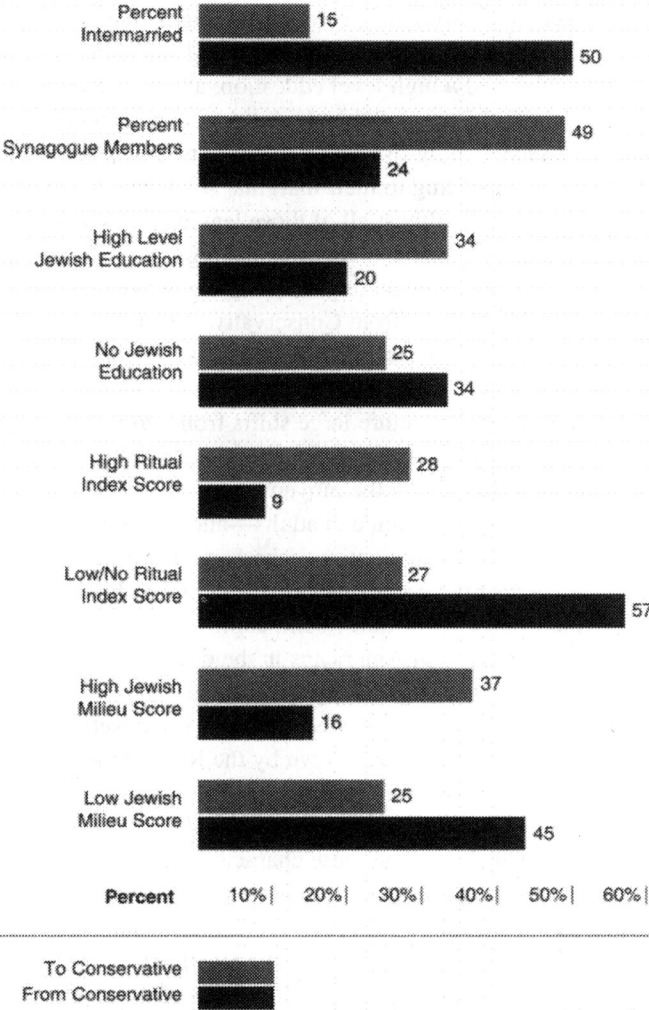

| | To Conservative |
| | From Conservative |

choice in this category. Overall, then, those joining the movement raised the Jewish educational level of Conservative Jews.

This reinforcement was enhanced by the level of Jewish education of many of those leaving Conservative Judaism, who tended to be somewhat less Jewishly educated than the stayers. For example, those switching to Reform were heavily concentrated in the two mid-level categories; compared to stayers, fewer had either no Jewish education or a high level. In sharp contrast, the small number of switchers to Reconstructionist Judaism were much more educated Jewishly than the stayers; more than half had a high level of Jewish education, and another 30 percent were in the medium category; few had no Jewish education. Reconstructionist Judaism thus seems to appeal particularly to well-educated Conservative Jews and may, in fact, be drawing off persons who might take leadership roles in the Conservative movement. Only one-fifth of those shifting to Just Jewish had a high level education, although a considerable proportion were in the medium level category. Not surprisingly, a majority of those switching to Other had either no Jewish education or only a low level. Attesting to their marginal status in relation to the Jewish community, almost all of those leaving Conservative Judaism to identify as non-Jews reported having had no Jewish education.

Together, these profiles of the Jewish educational levels of switchers to and from Conservative Judaism suggest that the movement has benefitted by the attraction of persons with higher-than-average Jewish education from each of the other denominations. In the absence of future large shifts from Orthodox Judaism, improvements in the educational levels of Conservative Jews will depend largely on the movement's success in educating its own members—children and adults—and in continuing to attract those from other denominations who have higher levels of Jewish education. Such a shift may be possible if traditional Judaism, as interpreted by the Conservative movement, comes to be seen as best fulfilling the needs of Jewish Americans in the decades ahead.

Ritual Observance. We noted earlier that Conservative Jews were intermediary between Orthodox and Reform in their level of ritual observance, as shown by the Ritual Index. We have also noted in our discussion of membership rates and Jewish education that those Conservative Jews who were also raised in the movement score somewhat lower on these characteristics than the total Conservative population. A similar relation appears when ritual practices are examined.

Persons joining the Conservative movement raised the level of observance of all Conservative Jews. One-third of those coming from Orthodox scored high, compared to only one-fifth of the stayers; and more were also in the medium category. Only 18 percent of the Orthodox switchers reported no or low levels of observance compared to 38 percent of those raised and remaining Conservative. The switchers from Orthodox Judaism have clearly brought a much stronger commitment to observance than that held by the stayers, whom they joined.

Similarly, more of those joining Conservative Judaism from a Reform origin scored high or medium on the Ritual Index, and fewer fell into one of the two lower level groups. Even those switching from Just Jewish showed such a pattern. They and those coming from Reform Judaism appear to have been attracted by the greater traditionalism in observance of the Conservative movement. The only group of switchers to Conservative Judaism to have lower levels of observance than the stayers is the Other group. They constitute an important target group for educational programs on the ideology and practices of Conservative Jewry.

Those switching out of Conservative Judaism are clearly persons who place less value on ritual observance and who largely follow the models provided by the group into which they have switched. Among the switchers to Reform Judaism, for example, only 8 percent scored high compared to 21 percent of the Conservative stayers and 25 percent of the Reform switchers to Conservative Judaism. Almost half of the switchers to Reform Judaism scored low or none; these scores were almost identical to the patterns of the Reform population as a whole. Those becoming Reconstructionist Jews were more observant than the switchers to Reform, but the proportion in the highest group was still below that of the Conservative stayers. The large majority of those switching to Reconstructionist Judaism scored medium. Overall, ritual observances are, thus, much more characteristic of the switchers to Reconstructionist Judaism than of the stayers in Conservative Judaism.

Not surprisingly, those Conservative Jews who became Just Jewish, those reclassified as Other, and especially those who became non-Jewish were the least observant. Nonetheless, observance of Hanukkah and attendance at Seder remain rituals observed by the respondents in these categories. Evidently, even among those becoming non-Jewish, family ties lead to some observance of Jewish ritual.

These data show that the level of ritual observance among Conservative Jews as a whole benefitted from the influx of switchers from all groups but the Other. By contrast, those leaving Conservative Judaism, with the exception of those becoming Reconstructionist Jews, were less observant or, at least, became less observant than the stayers upon joining another denomination or giving up their denominational identity. As with synagogue membership and Jewish education, these data point to the selective character of switching as an important factor affecting the Judaic profile of Conservative Jews.

Visits to Israel. Stayers and switchers can also be compared in terms of having visited Israel. While 37 percent of all Conservative Jews had visited Israel, this was true of 31 percent of those classified as Conservative stayers. The higher overall level of the total Conservative group again reflects the effect of switchers into the movement. Higher proportions among both Orthodox and Reform in-switchers reported having visited Israel. On this index of Jewish identity, as on synagogue membership, the in-switchers have provided a type of "Jewish blood transfusion" to the weaker expression of identity by the Conservative stayers. That the proportion for the Reform in-switchers is so high is especially notable because it is well above the percentage for the total Reform population. This suggests that the relatively small number of Reform switchers to Conservative Judaism have a particularly strong commitment to Judaism and serve, together with those coming from Orthodox Jewry, to strengthen the movement. On this index, the Just Jewish and, even more so, the Other do not score high.

Of those switching out of Conservative Judaism, only those joining the Reconstructionist movement had relatively more respondents who reported ever visiting Israel than did the stayers. The lower rates for all other groups of out-switchers point to weaker Jewish identity, consistent with the direction of their denominational change.

Jewish Milieu. Another perspective for comparing the strength and character of the Jewish identity of Conservative stayers and switchers is the type of Jewish environment in which respondents function, judged by the Jewish character of the neighborhood in which they live and the Jewish/non-Jewish composition of their friends. As in earlier analyses, these have been combined into a Jewish Milieu Index to facilitate comparison. Like our analyses of other Jewish identificational characteristics, the Jewish Milieu Index indicates that, on average, the switchers to Conservative Judaism score somewhat higher than the stayers. A large proportion of Orthodox switchers rated high on the Index; the Reform switchers were heavily concentrated in the medium category. Surprisingly, those shifting from Just Jewish had by far the highest proportion classified as functioning in a high Jewish milieu and the lowest proportion in a low Jewish milieu, suggesting that the Jewish environment may have contributed to their switch to Conservative Judaism. Consistent with earlier patterns, those shifting to Conservative Judaism from the Other group were largely concentrated in the low milieu category.

Except for the Reconstructionist Jews, the switchers from Conservative Judaism were operating in a considerably weaker Jewish milieu than the stayers or those switching in. Those shifting to Reconstructionist Judaism were on average characterized by a higher milieu score than the stayers; they included an especially high proportion in the medium category and fewer in the low group. All other groups of out-switchers were heavily concentrated in the low category. Either as a causal factor in foregoing their Conservative identity or as a matter of choice associated with their shift from being

Conservative, they are functioning in a largely non-Jewish environment, judged by neighborhood and friends. Overall, to the extent that informal processes, including Jewishness of neighborhood and Jewishness of associates, are indicative of strength of Jewish identity, these data on Jewish milieu suggest that neighborhood and friendship patterns are meaningfully related to the direction of switching, i.e., toward more or less traditional identities; over twice as many of all those switching to Conservative Judaism ranked high on the Jewish Milieu Index than did those switching out. Cause and effect is more difficult to determine. Some may move to more Jewish neighborhoods or seek Jewish friends because of their own practices and commitments to Conservative Judaism. Just as likely, and perhaps even more so, location in a Jewish milieu may increase the chances of making Jewish friends with strong Jewish identities and broad participation in Jewish activities, who, in turn, can influence others' behaviors and attitudes.

* * * * *

Our analysis of switching has shown the fluidity of denominational identification and has also helped to explain the relative stability of the size of Conservative Jewry. The large influx into the movement of some 650,900 persons who were not raised as Conservative Jews was countervailed by an out-flow of 727,900 persons who were raised as Conservative Jews. While most of those who switched into Conservative Judaism had been raised as Orthodox Jews, the majority of those switching out went to the Reform movement, signifying a general shift over time from more to less traditional forms of Judaism.

The in- and out-flows have had a substantial impact on the profile of Conservative Jewry at the end of the twentieth century. On average, switching has resulted in a somewhat older Conservative Jewry in 1990, and one more likely to live in family units without children. Switching out of Conservative Judaism is clearly related to intermarriage status: Out-switchers are disproportionately married to non-Jews. By contrast, in-switchers have low levels of intermarriage. The patterns suggest that a change in denomination is often an accompaniment to a change in marital status.

Most importantly for the vitality of the Conservative movement is the impact that shifts in denominational identification have had on Judaic characteristics and involvement. The Conservative movement has gained persons with higher levels of Jewish education, ritual observance, and synagogue membership. Conversely, those switching out have tended to be less Jewishly educated, to have lower levels of ritual observance, and to be less affiliated with synagogues. The net result has been to heighten the levels of identification of Conservative Jews.

Continuation of the past trend of interdenominational flows is unlikely. Just as American Jewry as a whole can no longer count on transfusions of Yiddishkeit from immigrants, Conservative Jewry can no longer count on large numbers of strongly committed Orthodox Jews to join the movement. It can, however, expect to continue losing members from among the more peripherally identified. This would have the effect of continuing to increase the level of commitment of those remaining, but it would also serve to reduce the size of Conservative Jewry. Such heightened commitment, and even augmented size, may also occur if Conservative Judaism can attract some of the more strongly identified persons from less traditional denominations.

VII. Current Realities and Their Implications for the Future

As a major denomination in American Jewish life, Conservative Judaism constitutes a critical dimension in the vitality of American Judaism as a whole. The Conservative movement developed over a century ago to help integrate the waves of East European immigrants into American life while enabling them to maintain their sense of ethnic and religious identity (Sklare, 1972). The movement was designed to preserve traditional Judaism in a form modified to fit more closely to American styles of worship and to be responsive to general societal changes. The success of the denomination within the framework of American Jewry testifies to the exceptional freedom that America has offered Jews to determine the content and form of their religious practices and behavior. Religious freedom for Jews in America has created a fluid, dynamic situation, both between and within denominations.

Since its inception, Conservative Judaism's response to the larger society within which it operates has led to changes in some of its religious positions as well as in its organizational format. These have included activities like men's clubs, youth groups, and social action organizations that fall outside the precinct of religious services and the development of religious schools. The Conservative movement's constituency has also changed, reflecting both general sociodemographic changes in the general American population and the flow into and out of the denomination of selected segments of Jews. As we move into the twenty-first century, continued responsiveness to the changing context is essential if Conservative Judaism is to retain its strength and numbers. A successful response requires obtaining a firm understanding of the current situation, delineating the demographic profile of Conservative Jews, and understanding their religious practices and attitudes. This study is intended to help establish such a basic understanding.

At both the national and the community level, an overwhelming majority of adult Jews, four in every five, identify themselves with one of the four religious denominations of American Judaism–Orthodox, Conservative, Reform, and Reconstructionist. An estimated 1,588,000 identified as Conservative Jews, constituting 35 percent of the total adult Jewish population. They were surpassed slightly by adults who indicated they were Reform. Orthodox Jewry constituted only 6 percent of Jewish adults, and Reconstructionist Jews just over 1 percent. Almost one in five reported that they were Just Jewish or

between that of Orthodox and Reform Jews. The same pattern characterizes ever having been to Israel and the importance attached to living in a Jewish milieu.

One additional, interesting insight provided by these data on denominational differences is the exceptionalism of Reconstructionist Jews. Since Reconstructionist Jewry constitutes less than 2 percent of the adult Jewish population in the United States (the movement is a relative newcomer on the denominational scene and has begun to grow only in the 1980s) and is still very small, its patterns can only be suggestive. However, on many indicators Reconstructionist Jews are more involved and more strongly Jewishly identified than their Conservative counterparts. For example, compared to Conservatives, they have somewhat higher levels of Jewish education, attend synagogue more regularly, and have higher levels of voluntarism and Jewish organizational membership. Since so many Reconstructionist Jews were raised as Conservative, this finding suggests that persons joining the Reconstructionist movement are selective of the more Jewishly identified and committed. Their leaving the Conservative ranks may, thereby, serve to somewhat weaken Conservative Judaism.

The Importance of Age

Previous studies of Jewish identification and commitment have pointed to the importance of generation status (Goldstein and Goldscheider, 1968). Strength of identity, as measured by a variety of indicators of behavior and attitude, diminished directly with distance from the immigrant generation. Since the immigrants had largely arrived in the decades around the turn of the twentieth century, this implied that younger persons were generally less observant and less involved in the Jewish community than older cohorts.

Another concern related specifically to age is the stance of the baby-boom generation. This exceptionally large cohort has had a profound effect on American institutions, from schools to political parties, and on the role of religion as well (Wertheimer, 1993). As they move into the later adult years and into retirement, they can be expected to again alter demands for services and affect the climate of opinion on a large number of important issues.

Cognizant of the importance of generation status and age, our analysis has included attention to age differences within the Conservative population. We find that the youngest group, those under age 45, is indeed furthest removed from immigrant origins and differs from the older groups in both sociodemographic characteristics and Jewish practices and involvement.

Among Conservative Jews, younger age is related to higher levels of education. Nonetheless, the younger males are no more likely to hold high white collar positions than those in the middle-aged group, and, in fact, are more likely to be found among clerical/sales and blue collar workers. Women aged 25-44 much more clearly reflect their high educational achievements. These women are heavily concentrated among professionals.

Almost one-quarter of the 18-44 age group is not married. And the young married, in sharp contrast to older respondents, are most likely to be living in households with children under age 15. Among those who are married, those married in the 1980s—i.e., largely younger respondents—were much more likely to be intermarried than those who married earlier. Concomitantly, attitudes supportive of intermarriage are inversely related to age—older Conservative Jews are less supportive than younger ones, except that more of the respondents aged 18-24 are opposed to intermarriage than those aged 25-44. Whether these younger persons represent a backlash against the more assimilationist attitudes of the somewhat older age cohort and also reflect the impact of better formal and informal Jewish education need monitoring.

Studies around the world have documented that migration is associated with those ages at which persons are obtaining higher education, entering the labor force, and entering the family formation stage of the life cycle. Younger Conservative Jews have been moving more often and longer distances at life-cycle stages that are particularly critical to their formation of ties to a given community and set of institutions. Since this group is also the most likely to have families with young children, moving may be especially disruptive to their children's Jewish education.

The youngest group of Conservative respondents is distinctive in having not only very high levels of secular education but also relatively higher levels of Jewish education. The notably low levels of the elderly are due in large part to the lack of women's Jewish education in the past. The higher levels of Jewish education among younger Conservatives do not, however, translate directly into higher levels of synagogue attendance, ritual observance, or involvement in the Jewish community. A smaller proportion of younger Conservative Jews reported that they often attended synagogue than was true of the older groups; they also had lower levels of ritual observance.

For a few practices, however, the very youngest group (aged 18-24) seems to have turned this trend around; their levels of seder attendance and lighting Hanukkah candles and even of maintaining kashrut are often as high as those of the older groups. Since some of these younger respondents are adult children living with their parents, the reported levels of household ritual practices may, in fact, reflect the practices of the older generation. For those younger respondents who have their own households, however, these patterns may augur a heightened level of ritual observance. Such behavior would be consistent with their higher levels of Jewish education and youth group/camp experiences. Apparently, younger people are choosing their ritual practices rather than following all of them as part of an overarching set of beliefs. Whether exposure to a more intensive Jewish education in the Solomon Schechter Day Schools will have a strong impact on this pattern remains to be seen as the growing number of Conservative day school graduates move into family-formation stages and develop households of their own.

Especially notable is the sharply lower level of community involvement of younger Conservative Jews. Membership in Jewish organizations, volunteering for Jewish activities, and contributing to Jewish causes are all lower among those aged 18-44 than among the two older cohorts. These patterns are echoed in two other measures of Jewish identity: having been to Israel and importance of Jewish milieu.

Conservative Jews who are under age 45 are clearly different from older respondents. Although more Jewishly educated, they seem to be quite selective about what they choose to observe and how they choose to identify with the Jewish community. They are much less connected to the formal institutional structure than are older Conservative Jews. Most of these patterns are quite likely related to life-cycle stage, in which case they may change as careers develop and family situations are altered. They may also reflect perceptions by some younger Conservative Jews that the formal institutional structure of the Jewish community is the domain of older, well-established Jews and that it has little room or tolerance for younger persons. Whether the patterns of these younger persons will change as they age warrants careful follow-up. The direction of change, if there is any, will have a strong effect on the strength of Conservative Judaism.

The Importance of Membership

Respondents' own perceptions and reporting have shown that nominal Conservative identification does not mean behavior that is in full accord with Conservative doctrine. Jews identifying themselves as Conservative cover a broad spectrum of behavior, from the very observant to those who are only marginally connected to Judaism. A more selective Conservative population, one that might be expected to act concretely on its identificational distinction, would refer to Conservative Jews who belong to a household in which one or more persons are affiliated with a synagogue. Just under half of all adult Conservative Jews live in such households.

Membership makes a dramatic difference in the profile of Conservative Jewry. Members tend to be older, married, and with children aged 15 and older living in the household. Conversely, nonmembers are more concentrated among the young, never married, or divorced. Clearly, synagogue affiliation is attractive to families and much less appealing to persons not in traditional family configurations. Among the married, intermarriage is sharply lower among members than among nonmembers—6 percent compared to 36 percent—suggesting either that nonmembers are much more predisposed to intermarriage because of their more marginal attachment to Judaism or that they do not feel welcome in a synagogue once they are intermarried.

Membership is clearly and unsurprisingly associated with much higher levels of ritual practices and involvement in the formal structure of the Jewish community. And members much more than nonmembers consider a Jewish milieu to be important for them. Especially strong differentials are also apparent in measures of community involvement, with members having much higher levels of Jewish organization membership, volunteering in Jewish activities, and giving to Jewish causes.

Since the affiliated Conservative Jews are the ones most visible to the Conservative leadership, their characteristics and behavior have often been assumed to be representative of Conservative Jewry as a whole. It is clearly misleading to make this assumption. Great variation exists between members and nonmembers. Nonmembers are significantly more marginal and, therefore, represent a population in need of outreach through special programming that appeals to younger persons, to those not in traditional families, to those who may be financially constrained, and to those alienated from the formal structure of the Jewish community. In his assessment of Conservative Judaism in the 1970s, Marshall Sklare (1972:260-61) suggested that all that was needed to further augment the primacy of Conservative Judaism was that nonmembers be induced to activate a commitment they already held. Apparently, the same problem remains two decades later. Whether Conservative Judaism can, in fact, draw these individuals into active participation remains a key question. It presents a particular challenge since the earlier large reservoir of potential members in the Orthodox community has diminished greatly.

The Geographic Factor

An important dynamic of the American population has been its redistribution across the continent. Jews have participated fully in this movement, so that the older areas of Jewish settlement in the Northeast and the Midwest now share more of the Jewish population with the South and the West. These major population shifts have been selective of Jews with certain characteristics and, in turn, have provided a

particular community context within which the Jews settled.
Reflecting the participation of Conservative Jews in this redistribution,
clear regional differences appear in their characteristics and behavior.
Not only are the differentials regionwide, but they also often apply to
individual communities, although the patterns are not as clear for the
more specific areas.

Lifetime migration patterns show the dramatic growth in the
population of Conservative Jews living in the South and the West. At
the same time, migration has not been unidirectional; all regions have
participated in exchanges with each other. In the process, regional
differences have been heightened; and migration has become an
important variable influencing the extent of integration into Jewish
community life.

Not surprisingly, Conservative Jews in the South, compared to
those in other regions, include a much higher proportion of elderly and
an exceptionally high percentage of households that consist of adults
only. The Midwest, with its relatively young population, has few
widowed, a very high proportion who have had postgraduate
education, and a disproportionately high percentage of male
professionals and female managers.

In general, the Conservative populations of the Northeast and
the Midwest are more traditional in their orientation and more strongly
Jewishly identified than are those in the South and the West.
Strikingly fewer in the West indicate that a Jewish milieu is of
importance to them. Intermarriage levels are especially high in the
West, where almost one-third report a mixed marriage. At the other
extreme, far more of those in the Midwest belong to Jewish
organizations and volunteer in Jewish activities.

An outstanding exception to the regional split is the percent
contributing to Jewish causes. Only small differences characterize the
four regions and not in the expected direction. Conservative Jews in
the West are just as likely as those in the Midwest to contribute; those
in the Northeast and the South are slightly less likely to do so.
Perhaps solicitation methods are equally effective in all regions;
perhaps those in the West prefer to show their identification through
monetary donations rather than through giving of their time or through
formal affiliations with the organized Jewish community. It is also
possible that giving opportunities within the Jewish community vary
more in the West so as to appeal better to its distinctive population.

The Dynamics of Choice
Geographic mobility among the Conservative population has been a
prominent factor in determining the current configuration of
Conservative Jewry. Other forms of mobility are important as well, in

particular the entry and exit of persons into and out of Conservative Judaism. Who is raised a Conservative Jew and remains one throughout the lifetime, who joins the movement, and who leaves all have a significant impact on the profile of Conservative Jewry.

Because the denominational identification for American Jews is a matter of choice, persons can easily switch from or into the Conservative movement or any of the other denominations, or out of all denominations altogether. Such changes may be a matter of religious belief, but more often other factors are salient. A switch may occur because one denomination is seen as a more "Americanized" or a more traditional form of religious worship; because only one or two options are available in a given community; because of convenience and proximity of facilities; because of marriage, family, or friendship networks; because switching is seen as part of upward social mobility; or because of a host of other reasons. While NJPS-1990 does not provide information on why or when denominational change occurred (or why it did not occur), it does allow some measure of that change. Questions asked of the respondent on denomination-raised and on current denomination permit us to identify the past denominational identification of persons who reported they were Conservative at the time of the survey and the current denomination (or lack thereof) of respondents who indicated they had been raised as Conservative Jews.

Information on denominational switching shows the fluidity of such identification. At the time of the 1990 survey, an estimated 1.588 million adults identified as Conservative Jews. Of these, some 917,000 reported that they had been raised Conservative and about 651,000 said they had not been raised as Conservative (for some, denomination raised was unknown). Another 728,000 indicated that they had been raised as Conservative but now identified otherwise. Thus, almost as many persons who were raised non-Conservative have become Conservative Jews as the number of persons who were raised as Conservative Jews but no longer identify with the movement. The result has been a net loss of about 77,000 persons for Conservative Judaism.

Examination of the losses and gains shows that the shifts have generally been from the more to the less traditional movements. The vast majority of the gains to Conservative Jewry have come from the Orthodox, while the largest losses have been to Reform Judaism. The shifting clearly has serious implications for the size of the Conservative movement, since the reservoir of Orthodox Jews, from which so many switchers into Conservative Judaism came, has shrunk sharply and is unlikely to provide the mass of population from which to draw in the future. By contrast, becoming Reform or Just Jewish, or moving out of Judaism altogether continues to be a viable option. The losses to Conservative Judaism identified by the situation in 1990 may thus continue into the twenty-first century unless the denomination is able either to retain its own membership or to attract members from other denominations or with no denominational identity.

The shifts have had a substantial impact on the profile of Conservative Jewry at the end of the twentieth century. Because much of the switching from Orthodox occurred several decades ago and switching to Reform is more recent, Conservative Jewry has become older. The in-switchers are disproportionately aged 65 and over and in households without children, but the out-switchers are more likely to be young adults with children under age 15. Because of these age differentials and because the in-switchers from the Orthodox were more likely to be immigrants or the children of the foreign born, those who adopted Conservative Judaism are somewhat less educated than the out-switchers, who are concentrated among the college-educated. Differences by occupation are less marked.

The data on intermarriage show that the in-switchers have particularly low levels of mixed marriages; notably more of the in-switchers are in conversionary marriages than is true of either the stayers or the out-switchers. In fact, half of the latter group are married to a non-Jewish spouse, and many of these no longer consider themselves Jewish. Our findings thus suggest that out-switching is often related to marriage; quite likely, it is directly the result of intermarriage. If intermarriage continues at the high levels characteristic of the 1985-90 marriage cohort, then losses can be expected to continue at equally high levels unless some kind of direct and successful intervention is developed.

Perhaps more important for the vitality of the movement is the impact that the shifts have had on those characteristics that relate to Jewish identification and involvement. The Conservative movement has gained persons with higher levels of Jewish education, ritual index scores, and Jewish milieu scores than those who had been Conservative Jews all their lives. The Orthodox pool from which so many of those who switched to Conservative Judaism are drawn has clearly had a strong, positive effect on the level of Jewish identity and behavior among Conservative Jews. On the other hand, those switching out of the movement have tended to be less Jewishly educated and to score lower on ritual practices and Jewish milieu. Persons who switched to Conservative Judaism also have higher levels of household synagogue membership than those who were constantly Conservative; the out-switchers were much less likely to belong to affiliated households. The net result has been to heighten the level of identification of Conservative Jews.

Continuation of the past trend of interdenominational flows into the future is unlikely. Just as American Jewry as a whole can no longer count on transfusions of Yiddishkeit from immigrants, Conservative Jewry can no longer count on the influx of large numbers of strongly committed Jews from Orthodox Judaism. It can, however, expect to continue losing members from among the more peripherally identified. This would have the effect of continuing to increase the level of commitment of those remaining if continuing members retain current levels of identification but it would also serve to reduce the size of Conservative Jewry. Such heightened commitment may also occur if Conservative Judaism attracts the more dedicated persons from less traditional denominations.

Entering the Twenty-First Century
Our analysis of the sociodemographic and Jewish characteristics of the Conservative population in 1990 points to several areas that will pose major challenges to the movement in the coming decades. These challenges must be seen within the broad framework of American society and changes in its attitudes toward and acceptance of religious diversity. The changes that have occurred in the latter half of the twentieth century have already profoundly affected how individuals relate to religious institutions and how they deal with private expressions of religiosity. Further transformations are inevitable.

At the most basic level, persons who identify themselves as Conservative Jews do not necessarily manifest this denominational identity by being members of households that belong to a Conservative or other synagogue. That more than half are in unaffiliated households suggests that concerted efforts may be necessary to reach this segment of the population. The reasons for their lack of institutional membership may well be conditioned by factors beyond their control — economic constraints or lack of a Conservative or other synagogue in the area where they live (especially if they have moved away from centers of Jewish concentration)—or by purely personal preferences. Better understanding of the dynamics involved in membership are essential for an understanding of why so many Jews who profess to be Conservative do not express their identity through membership, how to attract the unaffiliated, and how to retain those who are currently members. The generally low rate of affiliation among Conservative Jews and the selective characteristics of those who belong to synagogues also suggest that relying exclusively on studies of synagogues and their members may provide incomplete and possibly biased information about Conservative Jewry as a whole.

Conservative Jews vary widely in their religious practices, despite the overall halachic positions that Conservative Judaism has taken. This "pick-and-choose" approach to religion resembles that characterizing the general American population and even those Jews identifying as Orthodox. For Conservative Jews, the selectivity of practices may be exacerbated by the very nature of the movement. Conservative congregations have a great deal of autonomy in setting their own practices and formats, albeit within the confines of general Conservative ideology. Conservative congregations can, therefore, offer many entry points for individuals seeking affiliation. Moreover, since Conservative Judaism is seen as lying between the more traditional Orthodox and the more liberal Reform, many Jews may believe that, as Conservatives, they can personally opt toward one side or the other, choosing which practice suits them best at any given time.

The permeable nature of the lines between the major denominations and the large overlap in practices make it difficult to define a strictly Conservative position and may, thus, encourage individual choice. Individuals with widely varying practices and beliefs can feel comfortable within the Conservative movement. They can then respond to encouragement to be more observant of Conservative ideology at their own pace or not at all. At the same time, Conservative Judaism may also be attractive to Jews from other denominations or from the nondenominational segment who are seeking a more structured religious experience than is offered by Reform Judaism, but who are not generally halakhically observant.

Some of the vagueness within the Conservative leadership about matters of ideology that were identified by Sklare in the 1950s as a possible weakness remains. That the leadership is aware of the inconsistencies between ideology and practice is suggested by efforts to delineate more clearly for Conservative Jews just where Conservative Judaism stands on a wide variety of beliefs and practices. *Emet v'Emunah* was one step in this direction. More recently (May 1996) the Conservative movement issued a policy statement on intermarriage that clearly delineates the movement's position on that issue. Achieving a balance between the official ideology of the movement and the need and desire to be inclusive of Jews who do not necessarily subscribe to most of the stated positions is a major challenge for the Conservative movement.

Our analysis also makes clear that age is an important factor in determining individual religious behavior. In this respect, the baby-boom generation is of critical importance, most especially because of its size. As baby boomers move into middle age and beyond, their influence may have profound effects on the shape and content of Conservative Judaism. As they age and raise their children, their attitudes may change, and they may become more involved in matters Judaic. This may especially be the case if they or their children have been exposed to a Conservative day-school education and Jewish camping. Since both of these experiences are becoming more prevalent than in the past, they may have a strong impact on the future direction of Jewish involvement and identity.

There is little that the Conservative movement or the Jewish community as a whole can do to control the societal forces that have helped shape American Judaism. If large families are widely seen as a detriment to achieving personal life goals, then pro-family programs in the Jewish community will have little effect on raising the birthrate. Nonetheless, family support in the form of available child care, subsidized Jewish education for children beyond the first child in a family, scholarships for Jewish camps, and Israel incentive programs are all ways in which Conservative congregations can enhance the Jewishness of families.

If economic opportunities shift from one region or area of the country to another, most Conservative Jews, like other Jews and Americans generally, will tend to move to places where they can earn a better livelihood, regardless of the Jewish amenities that may or may not be present. Others will move in search of a more desirable physical environment, motivated by such concerns as climate and ecology. It becomes important, then, for the Conservative movement to be responsive to mobility both at the individual and institutional level. Especially useful would be programs designed to strengthen small and isolated Conservative congregations as well as support Jews living in areas where no congregations exist at all. Provision of visiting scholars and educators and dissemination of printed and electronic educational materials (such as video tapes and materials on the internet) are all ways to reach these communities and individuals. Facilitating transfer of membership from one Conservative congregation to another and/or of credit for initiation fees would enhance continuation of membership among mobile individuals. Welcome wagons sponsored by Conservative synagogues might also be useful, as would tracking of those who move, i.e., having the congregation of origin inform the Conservative congregation(s) at destination of the arrival of a new Conservative family/individual so that contact could be made quickly. A central data bank of members of Conservative congregations might be useful in coordinating such tracking. In this way, retention of Conservative Jews would be enhanced; and they would be helped to integrate into their new Jewish community quickly and more fully.

We have seen that in the past decades Conservative Jewry has lost adherents both to other denominations (especially to Reform and Reconstructionist Judaism) and out of Judaism altogether. Some of the losses are attributable to the appeal of less stringent practices and fewer demands on time and life styles. Many losses are the result of high levels of intermarriage, especially among the younger segments of the Conservative population. Whether these trends will continue at the same levels into the twenty-first century is difficult to predict. That they are likely to continue at least in the short run is quite likely. The challenge is to develop strategies for intervention.

Some of these strategies have been indicated above. Others might revolve about concerted efforts to intensify Jewish education at all levels, including both formal and informal experiences. The Orthodox emphasis on a vigorous and widespread day-school movement serves as one example. Full day-school education through the teen years may well help to retain the youth, particularly if it is coupled with stimulating youth group, camping, and Israel experiences. To be successful, however, day-school education must also involve the parents. Moreover, since a large segment of Conservative Jewry is unlikely to be able to or want to send their children to day schools, supplementary education must also be improved and synagogue family-education programs strengthened. Such efforts are already in place in some locations. Other congregations, including the smaller synagogues away from centers of large Jewish populations, must be strongly encouraged to institute similar programs. The national organizations of the Conservative movement may be especially helpful in this respect.

If the Conservative movement is seeking to retain its members, strengthen their Jewish identity and commitment to Conservative Judaism, and perhaps draw in those Jews who identify as Conservative but hold no formal synagogue affiliation, then it must develop programming that is able to be effective despite trends in the larger society. It must seek to speak to Conservative Jews—individuals and families—at a personal, meaningful level. A first step toward the realization of this goal is to know the characteristics of the constituency. The data from the 1990 National Jewish Population Survey have helped us to do so. A new National Jewish Population Survey planned for 2000 will provide new opportunities to assess Conservative Jewry and to evaluate changes since 1990. By identifying the sociodemographic and Jewish profile of Conservative Jews in relation to those identifying with other denominations, by recognizing the importance of both age and regional differentials, by distinguishing between members and nonmembers, and by examining the dynamics of change within the Conservative population, the important first step has been taken to establish the basis for making informed decisions about planning and programming.

References

Emet v'Emunah. New York: Jewish Theological Seminary of America, 1988.

Fishman, Sylvia, and Alice Goldstein. *Teach Your Children When They Are Young: Contemporary Jewish Education in the United States.* Research Report No. 10. Waltham, Mass.: Cohen Center for Modern Jewish Studies, Brandeis University, 1993.

Fowler, Floyd J. Jr. *1975 Community Survey: A Study of the Jewish Population of Greater Boston.* Research Report No. 8. Boston: Combined Jewish Philanthropies of Greater Boston, 1977.

Goldscheider, Calvin. *Jewish Continuity and Change: Emerging Patterns in America.* Bloomington: Indiana University Press, 1986.

Goldscheider, Calvin, and Sidney Goldstein. *The Jewish Community of Rhode Island: A Social and Demographic Survey, 1988.* Providence, R.I.: Jewish Federation of Rhode Island, 1988.

Goldstein, Alice, and Sylvia Fishman. *When They Are Grown They Will not Depart: Jewish Education and the Jewish Behavior of American Adults.* Research Report No.8. Waltham, Mass.: Cohen Center for Modern Jewish Studies, Brandeis University, 1993.

Goldstein, Sidney. "Profile of American Jewry: Insights from the 1990 National Jewish Population Survey." *American Jewish Year Book, 1992,* Vol. 92. Philadelphia: Jewish Publication Society of America, 1992.

Goldstein, Sidney, and Calvin Goldscheider. *Jewish Americans: Three Generations in a Jewish Community.* Englewood Cliffs, N.J.: Prentice-Hall, Inc., 1968.

Goldstein, Sidney, and Alice Goldstein. *Jews on the Move: Implications for Jewish Identity.* Albany: State University of New York Press, 1996.

Hartman, Moshe, and Harriet Hartman. *Gender Equality and American Jews.* Albany: State University of New York Press, 1996.

Hoge, Dean R., Benton Johnson, and Donald A. Luidens. *Vanishing Boundaries: The Religion of Mainline Protestant Baby Boomers.* Louisville, Ky.: Westminster, 1994.

Israel, Sherry. *Boston's Jewish Population: The 1985 CJP Demographic Study.* Boston: Combined Jewish Philanthropies of Greater Boston, 1987.

Klagsbrun, Francine. "3080 Broadway." *Moment* 12 (June 1987): 11-18.

Kosmin, Barry, et al. *Highlights of the CJF 1990 National Jewish Population Survey.* New York: Council of Jewish Federations, 1991.

Kosmin, Barry, and Seymour P. Lachman. *One Nation Under God: Religion in Contemporary American Society.* New York: Harmony Books, 1993.

Kosmin, Barry, and Paul Ritterband, eds. *Contemporary Jewish Philanthropy in America.* Savage, Md: Rowman and Littlefield, 1991.

Lazerwitz, Bernard, J. Alan Winter, Arnold Dashefsky, and Ephraim Tabory. *Jewish Choices: American Jewish Denominationalism.* New York: State University of New York Press, 1998.

Long, Larry. *Migration and Residential Mobility in the United States.* New York: Russell Sage Foundation, 1988.

Massarik, Fred, and Alvin Chenkin. "United States National Jewish Population Study: A First Report." *American Jewish Year Book,* 1973, Vol. 74. Philadelphia: Jewish Publication Society of America, 1973.

Rebhun, Uzi. "Trends in the Size of American Jewish Denominations: A Renewed Evaluation." *CCAR Journal: A Quarterly* (Winter 1993): 1-11.

Rimor, Mordechai, and Gary A. Tobin. "Jewish Fundraising and Jewish Identity." *In Changing Jewish Life: Service Delivery in the 1990s,* edited by Lawrence I. Sternberg, Gary A. Tobin, and Sylvia Barack Fishman, pp.33-54. New York: Greenwood Press, 1991.

Shapiro, Saul. "Survey: The State of Conservative Judaism." *United Synagogue Review* (Winter 1980): 8-10

Sidney Hollander Memorial Colloquium. *The Emergence of a Continental Jewish Community: Implications for Federations,* Collected Papers. New York: Council of Jewish Federations, 1987.

Sklare, Marshall. *Conservative Judaism.* New York: Schocken Books, 1972.

Waksberg, Joseph. "The Methodology of the National Jewish Population Survey," in *Jews on the Move*, by Sidney Goldstein and Alice Goldstein, pp. 333-359. Albany: State University of New York Press, 1996.

Wertheimer, Jack. *A People Divided: Judaism in Contemporary America*. New York: Basic Books, 1993.

Wertheimer, Jack. "Recent Trends in American Judaism," *American Jewish Year Book,* 1989, Vol. 89. Philadelphia: Jewish Publication Society of America, 1989.

Wertheimer, Jack, and Ariela Keysar. "The Geography of Conservative Judaism in the United States." In *Jewish Identity and Religious Commitment,* edited by Jack Wertheimer and Ariela Keysar, 5-11. New York: Ratner Center for the Study of Conservative Jewry, Jewish Theological Seminary of America, 1997.

Appendix A.
Methodological Issues

The data in this report are based on information collected in the 1990 National Jewish Population Survey (NJPS-1990). NJPS-1990 was the culmination of the work of the National Technical Advisory Committee on Jewish Population Statistics (NTAC), established by the Council of Jewish Federations (CJF) as a way to strengthen and standardize local community studies. In the 1970s and into the 1980s, assessments of Jewish life in America relied heavily on the findings of individual community studies. Although these yielded valuable insights, continuing concerns persisted about the accuracy and comprehensiveness of these studies and the conclusions about general trends drawn from them. The varied ways in which the samples were chosen—some based on Federation lists, some on distinctive Jewish names in city or telephone directories, some on area samples of more densely Jewish areas, and a few on random digit dialing alone or in combination with the other methods—gave rise to questions about representativeness. The quality and lack of standardization of the survey questionnaires and data analysis made comparisons among communities difficult, if not impossible.

These concerns, and especially the growing recognition that the Jewish community had become a national community (Sidney Hollander Colloquium, 1987), led CJF in 1988, following the recommendation of NTAC, to undertake a national Jewish population survey in 1990, to coincide with the national decennial census. In close coordination with Federation planners, NTAC designed the questionnaire to be used in the national survey; given the omnibus character of the survey and the limited time available for the telephone interviews, no particular topic could be covered in great depth. (For a broad summary of the NJPS-1990 methodology and findings, see Kosmin et al, 1991.)

The sample design was intended to ensure the widest possible coverage of the Jewish population, encompassing all types of Jews, from those strongly identifying as Jewish to those on the margins of the community or even outside it. It sought to include born Jews who no longer considered themselves Jewish and the non-Jewish spouses/partners and children of Jewish household members, as well as other non-Jewish members of the household.

A three-stage data collection process was employed to achieve a representative sample of about 2,500 households that included at least one person identified as currently Jewish or of Jewish background. The final interviewing, conducted in May-July 1990, yielded a total of

2,441 completed interviews with qualified adult (aged 18 and over) respondents, chosen randomly from among the household members who were Jewish by religion, considered themselves Jewish, or were born and/or raised Jewish. For these 2,441 respondents, information was collected on their sociodemographic, economic, and social characteristics and a wide array of attitudinal and behavioral variables related to Jewish identity. The survey instrument also collected less detailed information about the 6,514 members in the surveyed households, both Jews and non-Jews.

Appropriate weighting procedures were applied to the data so that the sample reflected the total United States population with respect to basic geographic/demographic strata, based on the U.S. Bureau of the Census statistics. The weighting procedure automatically adjusted for noncooperating households, for those who were not at home when the interviewer telephoned, and for households that did not have a telephone or had multiple lines. (See Waksberg, 1996, for a fuller discussion of the sampling and weighting procedures as well as a discussion of nonsampling errors and sampling variability.)

The weighted sample encompasses 8.1 million individuals. Of these, for analytic purposes, the Jewish core population consisted of three subgroups: (a) those born Jewish and reporting themselves as Jewish by religion; (b) the secular-ethnic Jews—those born Jewish but not reporting themselves as Jewish by religion and also not reporting any other religious identity; and (c) Jews by choice—those born non-Jewish formally converted to Judaism or simply choosing to regard themselves as Jewish. The peripheral population also consisted of three subgroups: (a) adults who were born or raised Jewish, but who had switched to another religion by the time of the survey; (b) persons who reported Jewish parentage, but who were raised from birth in another religion (some of these and those who switched religion still considered themselves Jewish by ethnicity or background); and (c) persons who were not and had never been identified as Jewish by religion or ethnic origin. Of the total households covered, 84 percent included at least one person identified as a core Jew; the remaining 16 percent were households that consisted of only those identified as peripheral population and included at least one person identified as Jewish by background or descent.

Of the vast array of information collected from the 2,441 respondents, several items are key to this analysis: whether the respondent considered him/herself Conservative, Orthodox, Reform, Reconstructionist, or something else; what was the denominational identification of the household in which the respondent was raised; the denominational identification of the household of which the respondent was a member in 1990; whether the respondent or any member of the household was currently a member of a synagogue or temple and, if so, its denominational identity; and, for those not currently affiliated or in nonaffiliated households, whether there had been earlier adult membership.

While most of our analysis used the national data for the Jewish population collected by NJPS-1990, we have also incorporated the results of several community studies to illustrate the range of variation that exists among communities. For this purpose, we have selected eight communities where population surveys were undertaken within five years of the national study. These are Boston, Rhode Island, New York City, South Broward, Columbus, Dallas, San Francisco, and Seattle. They were chosen to represent both large and medium communities and the four regions of the United States.

These community studies vary considerably in the population encompassed, the wording of questions, and the primary purpose of the study. Nonetheless, the studies are similar enough to allow their use for general comparative purposes. In doing so, we have examined only key variables; not all variables were encompassed by every community survey. The results of the community analyses were interspersed throughout our discussion of the national patterns to provide examples of similarities and differences from the national averages and to augment our assessment of regional differences among Conservative Jews.

The answers to many of the questions in the national as well as the local surveys, especially those related to denominational identity and religious practices, reflect a subjectivity factor on two levels. First, respondents applied their own interpretation to the questions, and, second. they replied in terms which were personally meaningful. Readers must be aware that respondents fit themselves into constructs and categories in terms of their own understanding, experience, and environment, rather than the official ideology of religious movements. This is particularly true of questions dealing with denominational identity and attitudes and practices that are inevitably more ambiguous than demographic characteristics such as age, education, and place of birth. In this context, we must accept the fact that in the United States religion and ethnicity are voluntary expressions of identity. Consequently, many people exhibit and report inconsistencies in their behavior and attitudes with respect to normative expectations, including those characterizing the various denominations. This analysis accepts their answers as reported. The readers and users of the analysis must decide for themselves whether to do likewise.

Appendix B.
Construction of Ritual Index

The Ritual Practices Index is a composite of five practices: Seder attendance, lighting Hanukah candles, lighting Shabbat candles, maintaining kashrut (defined as having separate dishes and buying kosher meat), and fasting on Yom Kippur. Since these practices vary in intensity, from once a year to daily observance, they were weighted differentially in the construction of the index.

*Seder attendance, lighting Hanukah candles, and fasting on Yom Kippur received a weight of 2 if performed always or usually, 1 if performed sometimes, and 0 if never performed.

* Lighting Shabbat candles was weighted 4 for always/usually, 2 for sometimes, and 0 for never.

*Kashrut was given a weight of 6 if respondent reported always/usually and 0 otherwise.

The index had a range of 16 to 0.

When tested through cross-tabulation by the denomination of respondent, the pattern was consistently in the expected direction. Orthodox respondents scored the highest, with two-thirds scoring in 9 to 16 range. Those reporting themselves to be just Jewish had the highest proportions scoring either 0 or 1 through 4.

It is not possible from the data set to disaggregate which ritual the respondent personally performs and which is performed by others in the household. Nor does it seem necessary to do so since correlations between pairs of rituals fall within a relatively narrow range (about .4000 and .6000), indicating that the individual-level ritual (fasting on Yom Kippur) is not differentially related to other rituals. The one exception is Kashrut, which has lower correlation values (between .1600 and .3000, except for a higher correlation with lighting Shabbat candles). It is, nonetheless, included in this study because Kashrut is an important form of normative behavior in Judaism despite the fact that it is not standard practice among Reform Jews.

Appendix C: Statistical Materials

Table 1	Denominational Identification of Adults and Their Synagogue Membership[1]

	Distribution by Denomination			Percent of Each Denomination Who Are Members
	Total	Members	Non-Members	
Conservative	35.0	47.0	28.3	46.5
Orthodox	6.1	10.7	3.4	61.4
Reform	38.0	35.3	39.4	32.4
Reconstructionist	1.3	2.0	0.9	50.7
Just Jewish	10.1	3.4	14.0	11.6
Other [2]	9.5	1.6	14.0	4.9
Total Percent	100.0	100.0	100.0	34.8

1. Synagogue/ temple membership in this and subsequent tables refers to household membership.

2. In this and subsequent tables, those who were classified as members of the core Jewish group but who also indicated that they currently identified with a non-Jewish religion or whose denominational identification was unknown are omitted from the tabulations. Unless otherwise specified, data are for adults only.

Table 2	Jewish Identify of Conservative Jews by Age			
Age	By Religion	Secular	By Choice	Total Percent
Distribution by Age				
18-24	9.2	14.1	-	
25-44	36.5	56.0	72.8	
45-64	25.0	14.5	19.5	
65 and over	29.3	15.5	7.7	
Total Percent	100.0	100.0	100.0	
Distribution by Identity				
18-24	90.8	9.2	-	100.0
25-44	84.5	8.6	6.9	100.0
45-64	93.4	3.6	3.0	100.0
65 and over	95.6	3.4	1.0	100.0
Total	90.7	5.9	3.4	100.0

Table 3 Current Denomination of Adults by Denominational Synagogue/Temple Membership of Their Households

(Only for those who hold membership)

Current Denomination	Denomination of Household						
	Conservative	Orthodox	Reform	Reconstructionist	Just Jewish	Other	Total
Conservative	83.3	3.4	9.3	0.9	1.0	2.1	100.0
Orthodox	10.4	86.7	-	-	1.0	2.0	100.0
Reform	3.4	1.3	88.5	-	2.5	4.3	100.0
Reconstructionist	*	*	*	*	*	*	100.0
Just Jewish	7.5	6.7	6.1	-	-	79.0	100.0
Other	-	-	21.0	-	-	79.0	100.0
Total	41.3	11.4	37.0	2.0	4.1	4.2	100.0

Table 4   Denominational Identification by Age[1]

	Conservative	Orthodox	Reform	Reconstructionist	Just Jewish	Other	Total
Distribution by Denomination							
0 - 5	6.7	11.7	9.1	12.3	10.8	14.9	9.7
6 - 17	13.8	19.8	14.9	18.7	12.9	15.5	14.8
18 - 24	5.0	6.0	3.6	1.7	7.2	8.4	5.1
25 - 44	32.5	24.2	41.0	43.3	35.8	41.4	36.3
45 - 64	17.5	10.5	17.6	22.4	16.2	14.7	16.6
65 and over	24.5	27.8	13.8	1.6	17.1	5.1	17.5
Total Percent	100.0	100.0	100.0	100.0	100.0	100.0	100.0
Median Age	40.1	35.3	35.9	33.0	35.7	30.4	30.2
Distribution by Age							
0 - 5	21.5	8.5	32.4	1.5	11.0	25.1	100.0
6 - 17	28.8	9.4	34.7	1.5	8.5	17.1	100.0
18 - 24	33.2	7.9	27.3	0.5	14.1	16.9	100.0
25 - 44	29.9	4.4	42.6	1.8	9.7	11.6	100.0
45 - 64	35.3	4.2	39.8	2.1	9.6	9.0	100.0
65 and over	46.8	10.5	30.0	0.1	9.6	3.0	100.0
Total	33.0	6.7	37.3	1.3	9.9	11.8	100.0

1. Children under age 18 were assigned the denomination of the household; adults' denominational identification refers to their reported current denomination.

Table 5	Age by Current Denomination and Synagogue Membership				
	Age Group				Total Percent
	18-24	25-44	45-64	65+	
Conservative	9.1	39.0	24.2	27.7	100.0
Member	9.9	33.1	26.7	30.3	100.0
Nonmember	8.4	44.7	21.6	25.3	100.0
Orthodox	10.8	34.4	17.7	37.0	100.0
Member	10.9	38.9	18.9	31.3	100.0
Nonmember	10.6	26.5	15.7	47.1	100.0
Reform	6.4	53.7	23.0	16.9	100.0
Member	9.7	44.4	26.5	19.3	100.0
Nonmember	4.1	59.0	21.2	15.8	100.0
Reconstructionist	5.4	54.0	38.4	2.2	100.0
Just Jewish	12.3	45.1	22.3	20.4	100.0

Table 6	Region of Residence by Denomination, and by Membership and Age of Conservative Jews

	Region of Residence				
	Northeast	Midwest	South	West	Total Percent
a. Denomination					
Conservative	44.8	10.2	24.8	20.1	100.0
Orthodox	70.0	8.0	10.9	11.1	100.0
Reform	40.5	12.4	23.4	23.7	100.0
Reconstructionist	37.3	21.3	16.2	25.2	100.0
Just Jewish	50.2	8.6	12.7	28.6	100.0
Other	35.3	11.8	25.8	27.1	100.0
Total	44.3	11.0	22.2	22.5	100.0
b. Conservative Jews					
Synagogue Membership					
Member	51.5	12.4	20.8	15.2	100.0
Nonmember	38.9	8.3	28.3	24.4	100.0
Age Group					
18-44	42.2	10.8	25.0	22.1	100.0
45-64	55.4	11.7	15.2	17.7	100.0
65 and over	41.2	8.1	31.4	19.3	100.0

Table 7 — Metropolitan Residence by Denomination, and by Membership and Age of Conservative Jews

	Central City	Central City County	Suburban County	Other Metro	Non-Metro	Total Percent
a. Denomination						
Conservative	53.1	21.2	14.6	6.7	4.5	100.0
Orthodox	74.5	9.0	8.2	3.8	4.4	100.0
Reform	51.1	22.8	15.4	7.4	3.3	100.0
Reconstructionist	50.6	25.0	24.4	-	-	100.0
Just Jewish	51.6	25.7	6.7	8.6	7.5	100.0
Other	50.3	19.0	18.7	2.9	9.1	100.0
Total	53.2	21.3	14.3	6.5	4.7	100.0
b. Conservative Jews						
Synagogue Membership						
Member	51.6	21.3	16.5	8.6	2.0	100.0
Nonmember	54.5	21.1	12.7	5.2	6.6	100.0
Age Group						
18-44	46.0	21.2	18.4	8.2	6.2	100.0
45-64	51.8	19.5	13.7	10.6	4.5	100.0
65 and over	64.1	22.6	9.5	1.9	1.9	100.0

| Table 8 | Generation Status[1] by Denomination, and by Membership and Age of Conservative Jews |

	No Grandparents Foreign-born	All Grandparents Foreign-born
a. Denomination		
Conservative	8.6	69.1
Orthodox	6.0	81.6
Reform	11.6	55.2
Reconstructionist	5.3	68.6
Just Jewish	13.7	61.5
Other	22.7	29.9
Total	11.4	60.2
b. Conservative Jews		
Synagogue Membership		
Member	7.9	72.5
Nonmember	9.3	66.4
Age Group		
18-44	15.1	47.5
45-64	4.1	80.7
65 and over	2.1	93.4

1. Only two categories of generation status—those with no foreign-born grandparents and those with four foreign-born grandparents—are shown in these tabulations. Persons with one to three foreign-born grandparents are omitted. The percentages therefore do not add to 100.0.

Table 9 — Life-cycle Stage by Denomination, and by Membership and Age of Conservative Jews

| | Life-Cycle Stage | | | | | |
| | One Person | | | Parent(s) with: | | |
	Under Age 45	Age 45 & Over	Adults Only	Children Under 15	Children 15 & Over	Total Percent
a. Denomination						
Conservative	10.6	16.3	35.3	21.9	15.8	100.0
Orthodox	8.3	24.2	28.9	28.8	9.8	100.0
Reform	10.3	13.5	34.3	29.4	12.5	100.0
Reconstructionist	20.5	4.2	47.0	23.7	4.6	100.0
Just Jewish	10.5	11.8	33.4	29.9	14.4	100.0
Other	13.7	9.0	30.0	36.6	10.7	100.0
Total	10.7	14.5	34.0	27.4	13.4	100.0
b. Conservative Jews						
Synagogue Membership						
Member	5.6	17.2	32.0	23.8	21.5	100.0
Nonmember	15.2	15.6	38.1	20.3	10.8	100.0
Age Group						
18-44	22.7	-	20.3	40.0	17.0	100.0
45-64	-	15.4	45.6	13.7	25.3	100.0
65 and over	-	41.9	50.5	0.5	7.2	100.0

Table 10 Marital Status by Denomination, and by Synagogue Membership and Marriage Cohort of conservative Jews

	Males					Females				
	Never Married	Married	Separated/ Divorced	Widowed	Total Percent	Never Married	Married	Separated/ Divorced	Widowed	Total Percent
a. Denomination										
Conservative	23.9	63.6	8.3	4.2	100.0	17.2	50.7	12.2	19.9	100.0
Orthodox	24.2	57.3	9.5	8.9	100.0	13.7	58.3	1.2	26.8	100.0
Reform	29.5	59.1	8.1	3.3	100.0	15.6	59.5	11.9	12.9	100.0
Reconstructionist	*	*	*	*	100.0	*	*	*	*	100.0
Just Jewish	18.4	66.1	8.9	6.5	100.0	30.9	48.5	12.1	8.5	100.0
Other	36.8	47.6	10.8	4.8	100.0	19.7	67.4	11.6	1.3	100.0
Total	26.5	60.3	8.9	4.4	100.0	18.2	55.5	12.0	14.3	100.0
b. Conservative Jews										
Synagogue Membership										
Member	15.5	72.5	5.1	6.9	100.0	15.3	53.9	9.3	21.6	100.0
Nonmember	31.2	55.8	11.2	1.9	100.0	18.9	47.9	14.8	18.4	100.0
Age Group										
18-44	43.7	45.2	11.1	-	100.0	35.4	51.1	12.1	1.4	100.0
45-64	3.1	85.9	8.9	2.1	100.0	5.0	68.0	21.8	5.2	100.0
65 and over	5.9	77.9	2.9	13.2	100.0	1.2	39.9	5.7	53.3	100.0

Table 11 — Intermarriage by Denomination, and by Membership and Marriage Cohort of Conservative Jews

	In Marriage	Conversionary	Mixed Marriage	Total Percent
a. Denomination				
Conservative	70.9	8.2	20.9	100.0
Orthodox	90.5	2.5	7.0	100.0
Reform	52.5	10.0	37.5	100.0
Reconstructionist	47.8	1.4	50.9	100.0
Just Jewish	41.5	4.5	54.0	100.0
Other	26.7	16.2	57.1	100.0
Total	58.6	8.6	32.8	100.0
b. Conservative Jews				
Synagogue Membership				
Member	84.8	9.4	5.8	100.0
Nonmember	56.7	7.0	36.3	100.0
Marriage Cohort				
Pre- 1980	82.8	5.0	12.2	100.0
1980-1984	46.3	15.3	38.3	100.0
1985-1990	40.6	14.8	44.6	100.0

Table 12 **Attitude Toward Intermarriage by Denomination, and by Membership and Age of Conservative Jews**

	Percent Opposed	Percent Supportive
a. Denomination		
Conservative	27.9	25.3
Orthodox	56.4	14.4
Reform	9.4	39.7
Reconstructionist	16.4	45.2
Just Jewish	7.2	47.0
Other	4.2	44.0
Total	28.1	34.3
b. Conservative Jews		
Synagogue Membership		
Member	35.4	20.2
Nonmember	21.4	29.7
Age Group		
18-24	31.8	35.5
25-44	23.9	29.6
45-64	33.4	22.1
65 and over	28.6	18.6

Table 13 Education by Denomination, and by Membership and Age of Conservative Jews (Persons Age 25 and Over)

	Education Completed				
	High School or Less	Some College	Completed College	Graduate	Total Percent
a. Denomination					
Conservative	32.4	19.7	23.0	24.9	100.0
Orthodox	42.5	12.4	25.2	19.9	100.0
Reform	14.6	25.7	31.5	28.1	100.0
Reconstructionist	11.2	5.5	23.3	60.0	100.0
Just Jewish	29.9	15.7	17.8	36.7	100.0
Other	23.0	29.8	26.5	20.8	100.0
Total	24.3	22.0	25.9	27.8	100.0
b. Conservative Jews					
Synagogue Membership					
Member	26.0	19.2	27.0	27.7	100.0
Nonmember	37.7	20.2	19.5	22.6	100.0
Age Group					
25-44	13.9	18.8	29.5	37.8	100.0
45-64	29.9	18.3	23.3	28.5	100.0
65 and Over	53.5	23.4	14.5	8.5	100.0

Table 14 Labor Force Status by Denomination, and by Membership and Age of Conservative Jews (Males)

	Labor Force Status						Total
	Employed	Unemployed	Student	Homemaker	Retired	Other	Percent
a. Denomination							
Conservative	66.5	4.7	5.7	0.5	21.5	1.1	100.0
Orthodox	53.4	0.8	6.8	-	25.8	13.2	100.0
Reform	76.8	4.1	4.9	-	11.1	3.1	100.0
Reconstructionist	*	*	*	*	*	*	100.0
Just Jewish	72.2	0.6	4.4	-	19.0	3.8	100.0
Other	73.5	4.3	10.2	-	8.1	3.8	100.0
Total	70.7	3.8	5.6	0.2	16.5	3.2	100.0
b. Conservative Jews							
Synagogue Membership							
Member	64.7	0.4	7.1	-	26.1	1.7	100.0
Nonmember	67.9	8.3	4.5	1.0	17.7	0.7	100.0
Age Group							
18-24	39.1	6.3	52.1	-	-	2.6	100.0
25-44	87.0	7.9	4.3	-	-	0.8	100.0
45-64	86.4	3.8	-	-	9.8	-	100.0
65 and over	25.8	-	1.3	1.8	68.8	2.2	100.0

*Fewer than 10 unweighted cases.

continued

Table 14 — Labor Force Status by Denomination, and by Membership and Age of Conservative Jews (Females) (continued)

| | Labor Force Status | | | | | | Total |
	Employed	Unemployed	Student	Homemaker	Retired	Other	Percent
a. Denomination							
Conservative	52.8	2.4	5.0	14.2	23.7	1.9	100.0
Orthodox	36.0	-	4.0	41.7	16.4	1.8	100.0
Reform	59.5	2.2	4.7	13.8	16.6	3.2	100.0
Reconstructionist	48.5	-	22.7	21.4	3.9	3.6	100.0
Just Jewish	60.6	1.9	6.4	16.4	13.3	1.3	100.0
Other	63.9	2.6	8.2	15.2	6.4	3.7	100.0
Total	56.2	2.1	5.5	15.9	17.6	2.6	100.0
b. Conservative Jews							
Synagogue Membership							
Member	47.6	3.2	7.2	16.3	23.7	1.9	100.0
Nonmember	57.3	1.7	3.0	12.5	23.7	1.9	100.0
Age Group							
18-24	43.8	-	56.2	-	-	-	100.0
25-44	79.7	0.9	3.5	13.8	-	2.2	100.0
45-64	66.6	2.6	-	16.3	9.6	5.0	100.0
65 and over	15.1	4.6	0.9	16.5	63.0	-	100.0

*Fewer than 10 unweighted cases.

127

Table 15	**Occupation by Denomination, and by Membership and Age of Conservative Jews**

	Occupation				
	Professional	Manager	Clerical/ Sales	Blue Collar	Total Percent
Males (Employed Persons Only)					
a. Denomination					
Conservative	42.2	18.3	25.1	14.4	100.0
Orthodox	47.3	9.8	21.0	21.8	100.0
Reform	39.1	18.8	31.1	10.9	100.0
Reconstructionist	*	*	*	*	*
Just Jewish	47.2	12.5	21.6	18.7	100.0
Other	48.2	9.2	17.2	25.3	100.0
Total	42.5	16.6	26.3	14.6	100.0
b. Conservative Jews					
Synagogue Membership					
Member	40.8	14.6	32.0	12.6	100.0
Nonmember	42.8	21.2	20.0	15.9	100.0
Age Group					
18-24	48.5	18.8	9.4	23.3	100.0
25-44	42.0	18.1	24.2	15.7	100.0
45-64	42.8	24.3	19.5	13.5	100.0
65 and over	39.1	2.3	52.0	6.6	100.0
Females (Employed Persons Only)					
a. Denomination					
Conservative	37.1	17.5	36.5	8.9	100.0
Orthodox	51.5	10.0	33.8	4.7	100.0
Reform	49.7	13.5	29.5	7.2	100.0
Reconstructionist	*	*	*	*	*
Just Jewish	39.5	16.6	32.9	11.1	100.0
Other	40.5	6.4	40.2	12.9	100.0
Total	45.4	14.2	32.3	8.1	100.0
b. Conservative Jews					
Synagogue Membership					
Member	35.2	22.0	38.9	3.9	100.0
Nonmember	38.5	14.1	34.6	12.8	100.0
Age Group					
18-24	6.2	14.8	53.8	25.1	100.0
25-44	48.5	15.4	26.8	9.3	100.0
45-64	25.7	30.9	37.1	6.3	100.0
65 and over	22.4	-	71.1	6.6	100.0

*Fewer than 10 unweighted cases

Table 16 Lifetime Migration by Denomination, and by Membership and Age of Conservative Jews

	Nonmigrant	Intrastate	Interstate Within Region	Interstate Between Regions	International	Total Percent
a. Denomination						
Conservative	15.1	25.3	13.1	36.4	10.2	100.0
Orthodox	32.3	18.4	8.9	12.0	28.4	100.0
Reform	18.9	23.9	15.0	36.8	5.4	100.0
Reconstructionist	9.6	17.4	24.6	45.4	3.0	100.0
Just Jewish	18.3	27.1	14.3	30.8	9.5	100.0
Other	15.5	23.1	22.6	33.2	5.6	100.0
Total	17.8	24.2	14.8	34.3	8.9	100.0
b. Conservative Jews						
Synagogue Membership						
Member	15.2	30.6	12.8	28.8	12.7	100.0
Nonmember	15.1	20.4	13.4	43.1	8.0	100.0
Age Group						
25-44	11.8	29.0	15.5	36.3	7.4	100.0
45-64	21.0	31.9	10.3	29.3	7.5	100.0
65 and Over	16.3	14.0	11.9	41.3	16.6	100.0

Table 17 Five-year Migration by Denomination, and by Membership and Age of Conservative Jews

	Nonmigrant	Intrastate	Interstate Within Region	Between Regions	International	Total Percent
a. Denomination						
Conservative	78.9	9.7	4.5	6.6	0.3	100.0
Orthodox	88.2	5.0	1.3	2.5	3.0	100.0
Reform	74.9	11.0	4.3	9.0	0.8	100.0
Reconstructionist	70.4	5.2	9.3	12.4	2.7	100.0
Just Jewish	73.6	15.8	3.5	6.8	0.3	100.0
Other	69.1	21.1	4.3	3.6	2.1	100.0
Total	76.3	11.5	4.3	7.0	0.8	100.0
b. Conservative Jews						
Synagogue Membership						
Member	80.8	9.8	3.1	5.9	0.4	100.0
Nonmember	77.1	9.6	5.7	7.4	0.2	100.0
Age Group						
25-44	64.5	16.6	7.3	11.1	0.6	100.0
45-64	91.2	3.6	1.9	3.3	-	100.0
65 and Over	92.0	3.6	1.3	3.1	-	100.0

Table 18   Anticipated Future Mobility by Denomination, and by Membership and Age of Conservative Jews

	Very Likely	Somewhat Likely	Not Likely	Total Percent
a. Denomination				
Conservative	21.1	23.2	55.6	100.0
Orthodox	18.8	15.2	66.0	100.0
Reform	26.6	20.5	52.9	100.0
Reconstructionist	27.6	14.0	58.4	100.0
Just Jewish	28.4	17.6	54.1	100.0
Other	34.4	19.9	45.7	100.0
Total	25.2	20.7	54.1	100.0
b. Conservative Jews				
Synagogue Membership				
Member	15.3	21.1	63.6	100.0
Nonmember	26.3	24.9	48.9	100.0
Age Group				
25-44	34.2	32.5	33.3	100.0
45-64	10.4	19.1	70.5	100.0
65 and Over	6.5	9.6	83.9	100.0

Table 19 — Index of Jewish Education by Denomination, and by Membership and Age of Conservative Jews

	Index of Jewish Education[1]				Total Percent
	None	Low	Medium	High	
a. Denomination					
Conservative	23.0	11.8	31.3	33.9	100.0
Orthodox	15.0	10.1	22.7	52.3	100.0
Reform	28.0	19.4	35.2	17.4	100.0
Reconstructionist	11.2	16.4	25.5	46.9	100.0
Just Jewish	44.5	16.9	24.4	14.2	100.0
Other	62.2	15.5	13.1	9.3	100.0
Total	30.1	15.5	29.8	24.6	100.0
b. Conservative Jews					
Synagogue Membership					
Member	13.3	10.9	31.0	44.8	100.0
Nonmember	31.4	12.6	31.4	24.6	100.0
Age Group					
18-44	17.7	10.0	29.9	42.4	100.0
45-64	17.2	14.5	33.9	34.3	100.0
65 and over	36.6	12.8	30.3	20.3	100.0

1. The categories of Jewish education are defined as follows: None = no Je
education; Low = 1- 2 years in any type of school; Medium = 3 or more year
Sunday school or 3-5 years of supplementary or day school; High = 6 or mo
years of supplementary or day school.

Table 20 Synagogue Attendance by Denomination, and by Membership and Age of Conservative Jews

	Attendance[1]				Total Percent
	Never	Seldom	Occasionally	Often	
a. Denomination					
Conservative	14.2	31.8	24.7	29.3	100.0
Orthodox	8.6	24.6	13.1	53.7	100.0
Reform	19.7	42.0	21.6	16.8	100.0
Reconstructionist	11.1	8.1	23.8	57.0	100.0
Just Jewish	45.7	36.2	11.2	6.9	100.0
Other	78.3	15.3	2.1	4.3	100.0
b. Conservative Jews					
Synagogue Membership					
Member	1.5	19.5	29.1	49.8	100.0
Nonmember	25.4	42.6	20.7	11.3	100.0
Age Group					
18-44	15.2	30.9	29.2	24.7	100.0
45-64	6.3	36.1	24.9	32.6	100.0
65 and over	18.5	30.4	17.6	33.5	100.0

1. Seldom = on High Holy Days or special occasions only; occasionally = several times a year; often = once a month or more.

Table 21 — Percent Performing Selected Ritual Practices[1] by Denomination, and by Membership and Age of Conservative Jews

	Sabbath Candles		Kashrut[2]		Fast on Yom Kippur		Attend Seder		Hanukah Candles	
	Yes	No	Yes	No	Yes	No	Yes	No	Yes	No
a. Denomination										
Conservative	23.2	48.8	14.7	85.3	70.2	29.8	73.7	11.5	72.8	15.4
Orthodox	51.4	29.6	60.1	39.9	85.1	14.9	72.5	7.3	77.1	8.7
Reform	10.1	67.0	2.1	97.9	51.7	48.3	69.5	11.0	65.8	18.1
Reconstructionist	22.6	54.1	8.8	91.2	81.9	18.1	80.6	6.9	70.4	17.6
Just Jewish	8.9	78.9	2.2	97.8	19.8	80.2	41.5	28.3	33.6	48.4
Other	3.0	90.9	1.7	98.3	5.7	94.3	20.4	63.7	15.7	72.7
Total	16.6	61.6	10.1	89.9	52.7	47.3	63.9	17.6	61.2	24.7
b. Conservative Jews										
Synagogue Membership										
Member	37.4	28.9	24.5	75.5	87.6	12.4	89.7	3.2	90.0	4.8
Nonmember	10.9	66.2	6.3	93.7	55.6	44.4	59.7	18.8	56.9	24.7
Age Group										
18-44	18.7	54.6	10.6	89.4	69.5	30.5	73.0	12.4	71.2	17.0
45-64	27.0	44.3	18.0	82.0	72.4	27.6	82.7	7.2	80.0	10.6
65 and over	26.8	44.3	18.0	82.0	69.9	30.1	68.2	13.5	69.5	16.8

1. Respondents answering "Always" or "Usually" are tabulated as Yes; those answering "Never" are tabulated as No. Not included in the data presented here are those who responded "sometimes."

2. Observing Kashrut was defined as always using separate dishes for meat and dairy foods and always buying kosher meat.

Table 22 Index of Ritual Practices by Denomination, and by Membership and Age of Conservative Jews

	Ritual Index Level				Total Percent
	None	Low	Medium	High	
a. Denomination					
Conservative	11.7	22.6	41.3	24.5	100.0
Orthodox	4.9	5.2	25.1	64.8	100.0
Reform	6.5	41.5	43.3	8.7	100.0
Reconstructionist	9.5	20.0	41.3	29.2	100.0
Just Jewish	21.1	58.8	15.3	4.7	100.0
Other	53.8	38.4	6.4	1.4	100.0
Total	11.4	34.9	37.3	16.4	100.0
b. Conservative Jews					
Synagogue Membership					
Member	-	8.2	49.1	42.7	100.0
Nonmember	20.9	33.9	35.1	10.1	100.0
Age Group					
18-44	6.3	24.7	48.4	20.6	100.0
45-64	4.8	17.7	47.1	30.5	100.0
65 and over	4.8	23.0	43.6	28.5	100.0

Table 23 Involvement in the Organized Jewish Community by Denomination, and by Membership and Age of Conservative Jev

	Percent Who...			
	Belong to One or More Jewish Organizations	Engage in Jewish Voluntarism	Contribute to Jewish Causes	Have Ever Been to Isr
a. Denomination				
Conservative	39.2	23.7	63.0	36.7
Orthodox	43.4	32.9	72.3	53.3
Reform	28.2	16.2	49.9	23.0
Reconstructionist	30.7	35.0	67.6	39.3
Just Jewish	14.9	9.6	37.9	21.0
Other	7.7	4.1	16.8	8.4
Total	29.8	18.3	51.6	28.3
b. Conservative Jews				
Synagogue Membership				
Member	57.6	39.1	79.5	49.0
Nonmember	23.4	10.6	49.2	26.2
Age Group				
18-44	30.7	21.3	49.5	30.6
45-64	44.5	27.4	73.1	36.3
65 and Over	48.4	24.0	77.5	46.0

Table 24 **Jewish Milieu Index by Denomination, and by Membership and Age of Conservative Jews**

| | Jewish Milieu Index | | | Total |
	Low	Medium	High	Percent
a. Denomination				
Conservative	27.9	37.2	34.8	100.0
Orthodox	17.8	30.9	51.3	100.0
Reform	41.1	43.2	15.7	100.0
Reconstructionist	21.6	58.4	20.0	100.0
Just Jewish	58.7	32.8	8.5	100.0
Other	77.6	19.5	3.0	100.0
Total	39.8	37.4	22.8	100.0
b. Conservative Jews				
Synagogue Membership				
Member	21.0	36.2	42.7	100.0
Nonmember	33.9	38.0	28.0	100.0
Age Group				
18-44	34.5	41.2	24.3	100.0
45-64	23.1	40.0	36.8	100.0
65 and Over	20.5	29.5	50.0	100.0

Table 25 · Lifetime Migration Experience of Adult Conservative Jews by Region

	Current Region of Residence				Total Percent
	Northeast	Midwest	South	West	
a. Lifetime Migration Status					
Nonmigrant	22.7	21.4	5.6	7.2	
Intrastate	37.4	30.9	6.7	18.8	
Interstate	29.4	37.3	77.0	65.5	
International	10.6	10.4	10.8	8.5	
Total Percent	100.0	100.0	100.0	100.0	

b. Lifetime Regional Redistribution (U.S. born only)

Region of Birth *Distribution by Current Residence*

Northeast	63.0	3.4	22.5	11.1	100.0
Midwest	9.6	42.2	11.6	36.6	100.0
South	21.5	4.1	64.8	9.7	100.0
West	4.2	6.3	16.7	72.8	100.0

Distribution by Region of Birth

Northeast	91.0	22.0	59.8	33.6
Midwest	3.5	67.9	7.8	28.0
South	4.6	3.9	25.6	4.3
West	0.9	6.3	6.9	34.1
Total Percent	100.0	100.0	100.0	100.0

Table 26 — Five-year Migration Experience of Adult Conservative Jews by Region

	Current Region of Residence				Total Percent
	Northeast	Midwest	South	West	
a. Five-Year Migration Status					
Nonmigrant	81.8	79.0	78.1	73.2	
Intrastate	9.8	10.1	6.3	13.4	
Interstate	8.4	10.9	14.9	12.7	
International			0.9	0.6	
Total Percent	100.0	100.0	100.0	100.0	

b. Five-Year Regional Redistribution (U.S. born only)

1985 Region of Residence	*Distribution by Current Residence*				
Northeast	94.2	0.9	3.1	1.7	100.0
Midwest	5.5	85.4	6.9	2.2	100.0
South	3.9	0.5	93.9	1.7	100.0
West	1.0	1.5	2.3	95.2	100.0
	Distribution by 1985 Region of Residence				
Northeast	96.2	4.1	5.9	4.0	
Midwest	1.3	91.9	3.1	1.2	
South	2.0	1.1	89.3	2.1	
West	0.4	2.9	1.8	92.8	
Total Percent	100.0	100.0	100.0	100.0	

Table 27 Metropolitan Residence of Conservative Jews by Region of Residence

	Northeast	Midwest	South	West
Central City	47.5	66.4	62.7	45.9
Central City County	16.8	17.6	13.7	41.8
Suburb	15.8	9.0	19.5	8.3
Other Metro	15.1	1.7	-	-
Nonmetropolitan	4.7	5.3	4.1	4.0
Total Percent	100.0	100.0	100.0	100.0

Table 28 Age of Conservative Jews by Region of Residence

	Northeast	Midwest	South	West	Total
0 - 5	5.5	9.0	8.4	6.5	6.7
6 - 17	11.6	17.5	10.8	18.9	13.8
18 - 24	5.5	5.1	4.5	4.7	5.0
25 - 44	31.3	31.7	33.9	33.6	32.5
45 - 64	22.6	18.7	10.9	14.3	17.5
65 and over	23.5	18.0	1.5	22.0	24.5
Total Percent	100.0	100.0	100.0	100.0	100.0
Median Age	42.5	36.6	40.5	36.8	40.1

Table 29   Socioeconomic Characteristics of Adult Conservative Jews by Region of Residence

	Northeast	Midwest	South	West
Life-cycle Stage				
One person unit > 45	10.6	8.5	12.2	9.9
One person unit 45 +	19.3	10.8	19.4	8.9
Two or more adults only	32.0	45.5	33.4	39.8
Parent(s) with:				
Children under age 15	18.3	26.7	21.5	28.1
Children age 15+ only	19.7	8.6	13.6	13.3
Total Percent	100.0	100.0	100.0	100.0
Marital Status				
Never married	22.2	23.8	17.2	18.1
Married	53.9	64.7	53.3	62.8
Separated/Divorced	9.6	6.7	15.1	8.4
Widowed	14.4	4.8	14.4	10.7
Total Percent	100.0	100.0	100.0	100.0
Intermarriage Status				
In-marriage	76.7	68.5	71.0	60.2
Conversionary	4.0	15.2	12.1	8.7
Mixed marriage	19.3	16.3	16.9	31.1
Total Percent	100.0	100.0	100.0	100.0
Education (persons aged 25 and over)				
High school or less	29.5	16.0	34.2	34.9
College	44.6	39.9	38.9	42.5
Postgraduate	25.9	44.1	26.9	22.6
Total Percent	100.0	100.0	100.0	100.0
Occupation (Persons in Labor Force only)				
Males				
Professional	42.8	46.7	39.0	42.9
Manager	24.3	18.8	5.4	22.0
Clerical/Sales	23.2	16.3	36.0	18.8
Blue Collar	9.8	18.2	19.6	16.2
Total Percent	100.0	100.0	100.0	100.0
Females				
Professional	38.1	26.2	39.7	38.5
Manager	19.8	32.0	6.9	14.6
Clerical/Sales	35.5	37.8	43.3	30.8
Blue Collar	6.6	4.0	10.1	16.1
Total Percent	100.0	100.0	100.0	100.0

Table 30	**Jewish Identificational Characteristics of Adult Conservative Jews by Region of Residence**			
	Northeast	Midwest	South	West
Jewish Education Index				
None	18.8	25.3	25.2	28.1
Low	12.8	7.5	12.2	11.3
Medium	32.7	33.0	29.9	29.2
High	35.7	34.3	32.7	31.3
Total Percent	100.0	100.0	100.0	100.0
Ritual Scale				
None	2.0	14.8	7.0	7.2
Low	18.0	7.0	30.5	32.3
Medium	49.8	53.5	39.3	44.6
High	30.2	24.7	23.2	15.9
Total Percent	100.0	100.0	100.0	100.0
Percent belonging to a Jewish organization	43.3	47.2	37.8	27.9
Percent in Jewish volunteer activity	22.2	45.5	23.8	16.1
Percent contributing to Jewish causes	57.5	61.0	57.7	61.4
Percent ever to Israel	37.1	38.4	42.5	31.2
Jewish Milieu Score				
Low	22.0	20.0	28.2	44.9
Medium	35.1	49.2	31.6	43.1
High	42.9	30.8	40.3	12.1
Total Percent	100.0	100.0	100.0	100.0

Table 31 Current Denomination by Denomination Raised[1] of Adult Respondents

Denomination Raised	Current Denomination						
	Conservative	Orthodox	Reform	Reconstructionist	Just Jewish	Other	All Denominations
Distribution by Denomination-Raised							
Conservative	58.0	3.0	24.2	45.4	17.4	16.7	33.9
Orthodox	32.5	88.9	11.8	15.6	14.4	2.7	23.4
Reform	3.9	0.7	55.5	17.5	13.2	22.8	26.2
Just Jewish	1.6	3.4	3.3	16.1	48.7	7.6	7.7
Other	2.5	2.5	2.2	5.4	4.2	40.6	6.0
Non-Jewish	1.5	1.5	3.0	-	2.1	9.7	2.8
Total Percent	100.0	100.0	100.0	100.0	100.0	100.0	100.0
Distribution by Current Denomination							Total Percent
Conservative	60.9	0.5	27.3	1.9	5.1	4.4	100.0
Orthodox	49.4	23.2	19.3	0.9	6.1	1.0	100.0
Reform	5.3	0.2	80.9	0.9	5.0	7.7	100.0
Just Jewish	7.4	2.8	16.0	0.9	63.9	8.9	100.0
Other	15.1	2.5	13.8	1.3	6.9	60.3	100.0
Non-Jewish	18.4	3.3	41.0	-	7.1	30.2	100.0
Total	35.7	6.1	38.2	1.4	9.8	8.8	100.0

1. Excludes those of unknown denomination raised.

Table 32	**Movement Into and Out of Conservative Judaism of Adult Respondents** (Denomination/Religion Raised Compared to Current Denomination/Religion)		
	Estimated Number Switching	Percent Distribution of Switchers	Net Gain/Loss for Conservatives
No change	916,770		
To Conservative from:			
Orthodox	492,400	75.6	+477,400
Reform	63,400	9.8	-365,700
Just Jewish	23,400	3.6	-59,900
Other	43,700	6.7	-32,600
Non-Jewish	28,000	4.3	-65,100
Total Gain	650,900	100.0	
From Conservative to:			
Orthodox	15,000	2.1	+477,400
Reform	429,100	58.9	-365,700
Reconstructionist	31,100	4.3	-31,100
Just Jewish	83,300	11.4	-59,900
Other	76,300	10.5	-32,600
Non-Jewish	93,100	12.8	-65,100
Total Loss	727,900	100.0	
Net change			-77,000
Total current Conservative population	1,588,100[1]		

1. Includes about 20,000 for whom information on denomination-raised is unknown.

Table 33 Changes in Denominational Identification of Adults from Denomination Raised to Current Denomination, by Socioeconomic Characteristics

	To Conservative from:					From Conservative to:				
	No Change	Orthodox	Reform	Just Jewish	Other	Reform	Reconstruc-tionist	Just Jewish	Other	Non-Jewish
Current Age										
18-24	9.3	1.2	7.3	-	4.0	3.0	-	13.4	-	11.7
25-34	22.9	7.5	35.1	-	12.3	15.8	39.6	24.2	15.3	23.0
35-44	26.0	13.4	19.9	31.5	39.9	29.8	43.7	42.4	36.8	23.2
45-64	21.8	23.9	18.9	47.8	31.2	30.6	12.3	14.8	37.1	30.5
65 and over	20.0	53.9	18.8	20.7	12.6	20.8	4.4	5.2	10.8	11.7
Total Percent	100.0	100.0	100.0	100.0	100.0	100.0	100.0	100.0	100.0	100.0
Life-cycle Stage										
One person unit >45	14.5	3.6	5.6	-	6.8	5.5	23.9	11.3	5.6	2.4
One person unit 45+	11.5	25.9	6.4	19.4	22.8	10.4	4.8	-	5.6	6.5
Two or more adults only	28.2	45.4	47.9	18.8	14.2	37.9	26.5	33.1	35.0	19.6
With children <15	27.1	14.1	22.0	31.5	37.5	29.4	44.9	40.1	36.8	47.0
With children 15+	18.7	10.9	18.1	30.3	18.8	16.9	-	15.5	16.9	24.5
Total Percent	100.0	100.0	100.0	100.0	100.0	100.0	100.0	100.0	100.0	100.0
Marital Status										
Never married	25.4	9.0	15.8	7.3	18.6	23.9	12.5	28.0	14.8	7.4
Married	52.7	61.4	70.4	67.5	52.0	64.0	81.6	62.9	79.8	63.9
Separated/Divorced	12.7	7.0	7.4	25.2	22.1	7.2	5.9	4.9	4.3	22.3
Widowed	9.1	22.6	6.4	-	7.2	4.9	-	4.2	1.1	6.5
Total Percent	100.0	100.0	100.0	100.0	100.0	100.0	100.0	100.0	100.0	100.0

continued

Table 33 Changes in Denominational Identification of Adults from Denomination Raised to Current Denomination, by Socioeconomic Characteristics (continued)

	To Conservative from:					From Conservative to:				
	No Change	Orthodox	Reform	Just Jewish	Other	Reform	Reconstructionist	Just Jewish	Other	Non-Jewish
Intermarriage										
In-marriage	69.3	79.2	82.5	*	17.0	65.2	*	39.8	-	-
Conversionary	4.8	5.5	-	*	61.8	6.6	*	5.2	7.3	-
Mixed Marriage	25.9	15.3	17.5	*	21.2	28.2	*	55.0	92.7	100.0
Total Percent	100.0	100.0	100.0	*	100.0	100.0	*	100.0	100.0	100.0
Generation Status										
4 grandp. US-born	11.0	2.5	14.8	7.3	56.4	75.2	84.0	61.6	45.7	32.8
No grandp. US-born	58.5	90.0	61.4	79.0	11.9	4.5	-	10.4	18.2	26.4
Education (aged 25 and over)										
High school or less	26.8	39.2	5.1	32.5	23.0	19.6	5.9	18.8	31.8	40.6
College	44.3	36.8	65.7	39.1	42.8	53.5	46.3	28.5	39.1	55.8
Postgraduate	28.9	24.0	29.2	28.4	34.2	27.0	47.8	52.7	29.2	3.6
Total Percent	100.0	100.0	100.0	100.0	100.0	100.0	100.0	100.0	100.0	100.0
Occupation (In labor force only)										
Professional	40.6	39.4	44.5	*	26.4	37.6	*	41.4	34.9	8.8
Manager	19.1	16.7	15.1	*	18.0	17.6	*	13.2	3.4	-
Clerical/Sales	27.1	32.9	40.4	*	48.0	35.7	*	26.3	47.5	40.1
Blue collar	13.2	11.0	-	*	7.6	9.2	*	19.1	14.2	51.1
Total Percent	100.0	100.0	100.0	100.0	100.0	100.0	100.0	100.0	100.0	100.0

Table 33 — Changes in Denominational Identification of Adults from Denomination Raised to Current Denomination, by Socioeconomic Characteristics (continued)

	To Conservative from:					From Conservative to:				
	No Change	Orthodox	Reform	Just Jewish	Other	Reform	Reconstructionist	Just Jewish	Other	Non-Jewish
Region of Current Residence										
Northeast	44.9	43.1	36.5	32.9	23.7	48.4	49.5	47.7	34.1	32.2
Midwest	11.2	8.0	14.9	19.9	19.1	8.5	7.1	13.0	6.9	20.0
South	24.4	28.5	33.8	18.6	31.0	23.4	10.3	11.3	45.0	23.0
West	19.4	20.3	14.7	38.6	26.2	19.7	33.1	28.0	14.0	21.8
Total Percent	100.0	100.0	100.0	100.0	100.0	100.0	100.0	100.0	100.0	100.0
Metropolitan Residence										
Center City	50.3	56.8	47.5	43.1	43.2	52.5	34.6	48.6	40.2	36.5
Center City Suburb	19.6	23.0	37.4	42.5	18.5	19.8	36.9	18.2	23.1	26.4
Suburban County	16.2	14.0	9.6	-	13.8	14.0	28.5	12.2	18.0	6.7
Other Metro	8.5	4.5	3.2	6.7	6.3	8.7	-	16.2	3.3	14.8
Nonmetro	5.4	1.7	2.3	7.7	18.1	5.0	-	4.8	15.4	15.7
Total Percent	100.0	100.0	100.0	100.0	100.0	100.0	100.0	100.0	100.0	100.0

Note: Switchers from Conservative to Orthodox are omitted because the category includes fewer than 10 unweighted cases.
*Fewer than 10 unweighted cases

Table 34 Lifetime Migration Experience by Changes in Denominational Identification

	Migrated	Migrated Interstate	Migrated Interregionally
No change	83.2	52.8	35.9
To Conservative from:			
Orthodox	79.7	56.2	45.9
Reform	98.0	69.6	54.3
Just Jewish	*	*	*
Other	86.0	45.9	29.0
From Conservative to:			
Orthodox	*	*	*
Reform	81.1	51.7	40.6
Reconstructionist	100.0	53.8	29.5
Just Jewish	88.4	58.9	44.4
Other	88.9	57.1	30.2
Non-Jewish	80.3	31.0	18.0

*Fewer than 10 unweighted cases.

Table 35 Changes in Denominational Identification of Adults from Denomination Raised to Current Denomination, by Selected Jewish Identificational Characteristics

	No Change	To Conservative from:				From Conservative to:				
		Orthodox	Reform	Just Jewish	Other	Reform	Reconstruc- tionist	Just Jewish	Other	Non- Jewish
Synagogue Membership										
Yes	38.7	53.0	54.5	42.6	30.4	34.7	36.8	14.9	1.0	0.0
Jewish Education										
None	31.9	16.3	21.6	30.9	65.7	23.5	4.3	23.7	43.1	92.0
Low	9.6	11.5	13.6	6.6	20.5	20.1	14.1	11.6	15.6	-
Medium	29.8	30.0	42.0	31.5	11.8	33.2	29.9	45.4	26.2	8.0
High	28.7	42.2	22.8	30.9	2.1	23.2	51.7	19.3	15.1	-
Ritual Index										
None	11.1	3.3	7.6	12.0	34.3	5.9	-	10.0	45.4	63.1
Low	27.3	14.7	15.5	5.6	32.1	39.4	4.5	63.1	49.0	22.6
Medium	41.0	49.2	51.7	42.8	24.6	46.2	79.1	18.9	4.5	7.3
High	20.6	32.8	25.3	39.5	9.0	8.4	16.5	8.0	1.0	7.0
Percent Ever to Israel	31.1	42.6	51.0	22.4	7.5	27.4	41.2	21.7	15.5	4.9
Jewish Milieu										
Low	35.8	21.4	13.3	6.2	57.8	30.9	28.6	58.5	77.5	79.3
Medium	35.1	36.1	59.4	36.6	32.8	46.7	41.6	38.2	21.5	20.8
High	29.2	42.4	27.3	57.2	9.3	22.5	29.8	3.3	1.1	-

| Table A | Estimated Population Size of Major Denominations, by Membership Status |

	Children 0 - 17[1]	Adults[2]	Total
Total Identifying with Denomination			
Conservative	270,000	1,588,000	1,858,000
Orthodox	95,000	275,000	370,000
Reform	353,000	1,722,000	2,075,000
Persons in Households with Membership			
Conservative	175,000	772,000	947,000
Orthodox	80,000	176,000	256,000
Reform	206,000	581,000	787,000
Persons in Households with No Membership			
Conservative	95,000	816,000	911,000
Orthodox	15,000	99,000	114,000
Reform	147,000	1,131,000	1,278,000
Percent who are Members			
Conservative	65	48	51
Orthodox	84	64	69
Reform	58	34	38

1. Denomination of children is based on denomination of household in which they live.
2. Denomination of adults is based on self-identification of respondent.

Table B — Selected Characteristics of Conservative Jews, Selected Communities

	Boston 1985	Rhode Island 1987	New York 1991	South Broward 1990	Columbus 1990	Dallas 1987	San Francisco 1987	Seattle 1990
Distribution by Denomination								
Conservative	38	47	34	39	33	34	20	20
Orthodox	6	7	14	6	13	4	3	8
Reform	41	32	37	28	47	49	43	37
Reconstruction	2	0.4	2	-	3	-	1	-
Just-Jewish/Other	13	13	13	27	4	13	33	35
Total Percent	100	100	100	100	100	100	100.0	100.0
Adult Age Distribution								
18-44	44	30	47	16	56	60	55	47
45-64	36	34	30	23	27	24	28	34
65 and over	20	36	23	61	17	16	17	19
Marital Status								
Never Married	21	7	19	4	19	19	20	8
Married	64	71	61	53	66	64	64	73
Separated/Divorced	6	6	9	8	7	10	9	6
Widowed	9	16	11	35	8	7	7	13
Education (age 25+)								
High School or Less	39	30	22	45	13	14	12	13
College	45	42	49	38	54	58	46	30
Postgraduate	16	28	29	17	33	28	42	57

continued

Table B **Selected Characteristics of Conservative Jews, Selected Communities** (continued)

	Boston 1985	Rhode Island 1987	New York 1991	South Broward 1990	Columbus 1990	Dallas 1987	San Francisco 1987	Seattle 1990
Generation Status								
4 Grandparents Foreign-born	76	66	76	93	43	67	NA	73
4 Grandparents US-born	5	4	4	2	15	9	NA	1
Employment Status								
In Labor Force	71	55	64	23	72	74	NA	73
Homemaker	9	14	19	13	10	12		7
Retired	16	28	9	62	13	13		19
Other	4	3	8	2	5	1		1
Occupation (Employed Only)								
Professional	45	40	48	34	54	33	35	45
Manager	20	21	19	22	17	24	31	12
Clerical/Sales	28	31	24	40	18	35	26	39
Blue Collar	7	8	9	4	11	8	8	4
Lifetime Migration								
Nonmigrant	38	13	14	0.3	29	15	10	41
Intrastate	24	37	64[1]	1	23	10	9	7
Interstate	30	40	10	79	40	63	60	40
International	8	10	12	20	8	12	21	12

continued

Table B Selected Characteristics of Conservative Jews, Selected Communities (continued)

	Boston 1985	Rhode Island 1987	New York 1991	South Broward 1990	Columbus 1990	Dallas 1987	San Francisco 1987	Seattle 1990
Five-Year Migration								
Nonmigrant	82	84	27	79	87	63	78	67
Intrastate	10	10	73	8	4	9	7	16 [2]
Interstate	7	6	-	13	7	26	12	17
International	1	0.2	-	0.3	2	2	3	-
Percent Synagogue/Temple								
Members	67	81	52	53	76	65	50	54
Percent Intermarried	4	NA	8	2	11	8	10	5
Percent Belonging to Jewish Organizations	64	61	33	35	NA	60	48	48
Percent Engaged in Jewish Voluntarism	34	37	40	33	40	44	35	44
Percent Contributing to Jewish Causes	99	96	72	81	72	78	72	69
Ritual Scale								
None	1	27	1	4	1	1	1	-
Low	71	-	18	13	18	12	17	17
Medium	-	42	41	46	69	74	67	64
High	28	31	41	38	12	13	15	19
Percent Ever to Israel	48	50	43	59	47	46	60	44

1. Any move into borough.
2. Seattle intermarried includes Jews married to non-Jews; it does not include Jews married to persons with no religion (22%).

Table C — Changes in Denominational Identification of Adults Moving Into and Out of Conservative Judaism, By Socioeconomic Characteristics

	No Change	To Conservative	From Conservative
Current Age			
18-24	9.3	2.1	4.9
25-34	22.9	10.4	19.9
35-44	26.0	18.8	31.4
45-64	21.8	25.4	28.3
65 and over	20.0	43.3	15.6
Total Percent	100.0	100.0	100.0
Life-cycle Stage			
Single <45	14.5	4.1	6.8
Single 45+	11.5	23.5	7.7
Adults only	28.2	40.0	33.6
With children <15	27.1	19.0	34.6
With children 15+	18.7	13.4	17.2
Total Percent	100.0	100.0	100.0
Marital Status			
Never married	25.4	11.1	15.4
Married	52.7	61.3	68.3
Separated/Divorced	12.7	10.1	11.9
Widowed	9.1	17.5	4.4
Total Percent	100.0	100.0	100.0
Intermarriage			
In-marriage	69.3	72.2	44.4
Conversionary	4.8	12.6	5.3
Mixed Marriage	25.9	15.2	50.3[1]
Total Percent	100.0	100.0	100.0
Generation Status			
4 grandp US-born	11.0	12.1	64.9
No grandp US-born	58.5	75.0	9.3
Region of Current Residence			
Northeast	44.9	39.2	44.3
Midwest	11.2	10.4	10.1
South	24.4	29.0	24.2
West	19.4	21.4	21.4
Total Percent	100.0	100.0	100.0
Education			
High school or less	26.8	34.6	22.6
College	44.3	39.9	49.2
Postgraduate	28.9	25.5	28.2
Total Percent	100.0	100.0	100.0

continued

About the Authors

SIDNEY GOLDSTEIN is George Hazard Crooker University Professor Emeritus and Professor Emeritus of Sociology at Brown University. He served as Director of the University's Population Studies and Training Center for 25 years, and is a former President of the Population Association of America. His research has focused both on nations in Asia and Africa and on the Jewish population of the United States and Lithuania. Considered the dean of Jewish population studies, he has played a key role in the development of national and local Jewish population studies. He is an active member of the Jewish community of Rhode Island.

ALICE GOLDSTEIN is a Research Associate at Brown University's Population Studies and Training Center. Her research interests include the demographic situation in China and Vietnam, as well as the situation of American Jewry. Using both local and national data, she has been concerned particularly with women's roles, philanthropy, and education and their relation to Jewish identity. She is active in a number of Jewish organizations, nationally and in Rhode Island, and is a past president of the Bureau of Jewish Education of Rhode Island.

Table C — Changes in Denominational Identification of Adults Moving Into and Out of Conservative Judaism, By Socioeconomic Characteristics (continued)

	No Change	To Conservative	From Conservative
Occupation (For those in labor force only)			
Professional	40.6	38.9	34.0
Manager	19.1	15.9	13.4
Clerical/Sales	27.1	35.7	37.4
Blue Collar	13.2	9.5	15.2
Total Percent	100.0	100.0	100.0
Metropolitan Residence			
Center City	50.3	53.4	47.5
Center City Suburb	19.6	24.2	22.0
Suburban County	16.2	13.1	14.2
Other Metro	8.5	4.7	8.9
Non-Metro	5.4	4.6	7.3
Total Percent	100.0	100.0	100.0
Percent Synagogue Members	38.7	49.3	24.0
Jewish Education			
None	31.9	24.6	33.6
Low	9.6	12.8	15.3
Medium	29.8	28.4	30.9
High	28.7	34.2	20.2
Total Percent	100.0	100.0	100.0
Ritual Index			
None	11.1	9.2	18.3
Low	27.3	17.3	39.0
Medium	41.0	45.1	34.0
High	20.6	28.4	8.6
Total Percent	100.0	100.0	100.0
Percent Ever to Israel	31.1	37.2	24.4
Jewish Milieu			
Low	35.8	25.8	44.6
Medium	35.1	37.6	39.2
High	29.2	36.6	16.1
Total Percent	100.0	100.0	100.0

1. 52 percent of respondents who switched from Conservative and are included in the mixed-married category identified as Non-Jews at the time of the survey.

www.ingramcontent.com/pod-product-compliance
Lightning Source LLC
Chambersburg PA
CBHW051837090426
42736CB00011B/1854